Candide

Candide

or Optimism

∽

Translated from the German of Dr. Ralph
with additions found in the doctor's pocket when he died,
at Minden, in the year of our Lord 1759

Voltaire

Translated by Burton Raffel

Yale University Press   New Haven & London

Designed by Rebecca Gibb. Set in Fournier type by Keystone Typesetting, Inc.
Printed in the United States of America.

Library of Congress Cataloging-in-Publication Data

Voltaire, 1694–1778
[Candide, English]
Candide, or Optimism / Voltaire ; translated by Burton Raffel.
p.   cm.
Includes bibliographical references.
ISBN 0-300-10655-6 (clothbound : alk. paper)
I. Title: Candide. II. Title: Optimism. III. Raffel, Burton. IV. Title.
PQ2082.C3E5 2005b
843'.5—dc22
2004022916

A catalogue record for this book is available from the British Library.

The paper in this book meets the guidelines for permanence and durability of the
Committee on Production Guidelines for Book Longevity of the Council on Library
Resources.

10 9 8 7 6 5 4 3 2 1

For Amy Raffel

CONTENTS

INTRODUCTION

Candide, Voltaire, and the Enlightenment

Johnson Kent Wright

As Burton Raffel remarks in the prefatory note to his sparkling new translation, *Candide* has been "compulsory reading" for nearly two hundred and fifty years now. At first glance, the explanation for this staying power seems obvious. It clearly reflects *Candide*'s undiminished capacity to move, delight, and instruct its readers, according to the classical maxim. Yet it remains to explain exactly *how* Voltaire's novella still manages this feat, so long after the world in and for which it was written has passed away. For *Candide* is a satire—one of the most celebrated examples of the genre in modern literature—and satire, no matter how captivating at the time, has a notoriously short shelf-life, once its object and moment have passed. What has kept Voltaire's lampoon of eighteenth-century philosophic "optimism" so fresh and so engaging, after all these years? Raffel rightly suggests that the answer lies in the *universality* of Voltaire's themes—the sense that we still recognize ourselves in the mirror of his characters and their concerns, as if we would not be surprised to encounter Candide or Cunégonde on the streets of Manhattan today. Paradoxically, however, any attempt to explain this sense of familiarity and currency must return us to the very particular context in which *Candide* was produced—above all, to the intersection between an unprecedented intellectual movement and an extraordinary individual life.

The movement was the Enlightenment, the great revolt against inherited intellectual authority—classical and Christian alike—that swept across Europe in the eighteenth century. Its seeds can be traced to a set of intrepid thinkers from the middle of the preceding century: the major figures of what was later called the Scientific Revolution—Galileo Galilei, William Harvey, and Isaac Newton; philosophers such as René Descartes, Benedict de Spinoza, and Gottfried Leibniz; and theorists of "natural rights"—Hugo Grotius, Thomas Hobbes, and John Locke. It is no accident that most of these came from or lived in either England or the Dutch Republic, countries that had succeeded in overthrowing the rule of divine-right or absolute monarchy in the course of the seventeenth century. Nor is it surprising that their ideas began to make their way into France early in the eighteenth, when that nation was in recovery from the long and exhausting reign of the greatest of all absolute monarchs, Louis XIV. For this was what the Enlightenment amounted to, in the first instance: the process by which French thinkers translated and popularized the ideas of their more advanced Dutch and English predecessors, for presentation to a far wider audience than they had ever reached before. These ideas never formed a single coherent doctrine. But by the time the Enlightenment reached its maturity, in the middle years of the century, there was a rough consensus among its leading thinkers in regard to certain key themes: rejection of orthodox, scriptural Christianity, in favor of deism or natural reli-

gion; conviction of the superiority of modern over ancient thought, above all owing to recent achievements in the natural sciences; extension of this natural-scientific model to a host of new social sciences, including economics, psychology, and sociology; and a proto-liberal political program, aimed at protecting what were now seen as the equal natural rights of individuals. The most famous vehicle for the propagation of these ideas was, of course, the great collective enterprise of the *Encyclopedia* edited by Jean le Rond d'Alembert and Denis Diderot between 1751 and 1772. But it is also striking how easily the themes of the Enlightenment lent themselves to expression in imaginative literature. The French Enlightenment was in fact launched with an epistolary novel, the Baron de Montesquieu's dazzling *Persian Letters* (1722), which held up a critical mirror to European society by recounting the visit of two Muslims to France. A little over a half-century later, the Enlightenment closed, in a sense, with the supreme expression of its cosmopolitan and egalitarian
. values, Wolfgang Amadeus Mozart's opera *The Marriage of Figaro* (1786)—the joint product of a French Protestant, an Italian Jew, and an Austrian Catholic.

But of all the literature and art associated with the Enlightenment, none has had quite the success of *Candide*. It literally flew off the presses at the moment of its publication in early 1759, appearing almost immediately in multiple editions in every European language, eventually selling more copies than any other eighteenth-century book. Today, two and a half centuries later, it has a wider readership than ever, one that is almost certainly still increasing—not least because of the historical shorthand that has turned it into a veritable icon of the Enlightenment. How did it happen that this one novella managed to capture the essence of this large and complicated intellectual movement?

The achievement has everything to do with the remarkable career of its author, who, more than a mere "writer," was in many ways the first *intellectual* of the modern world, a social role he virtually invented. He was born François-Marie Arouet in Paris on November 21, 1694, the son of a lawyer and banker prosperous enough to furnish him with an education at the finest Jesuit school of the time — where, Voltaire later claimed, he was also sexually abused by his warders. By his mid-twenties, he had abandoned the legal career chosen by his family for a life of letters, rapidly establishing a reputation as a leading dramatist and poet. By this point, he had also discarded his patronymic, adopting as a pen name an anagram of Arouet (with *le jeune*, "the younger") that echoed the French verb *volter*, "to turn abruptly." Nimbleness was a useful trait, given Voltaire's chafing against the social constraints that a bourgeois poet naturally encountered in the aristocratic world of regency France. His satirical verse already landed him in the famous Bastille prison in 1717–18. A more serious run-in with a petty noble in 1726 led to a severe beating on the streets of Paris, another stint in the Bastille, and then prudent exile in England.

The two years Voltaire spent there were a first turning point in his life. For in England, he encountered a society that was not only very different from that of France, but one that seemed more *advanced*, in every respect—freer and more tolerant, richer and more rational. The result was an enthusiastic traveler's report, *Letters Concerning the English Nation* (1733), which in one stroke placed Voltaire at the forefront of the early Enlightenment. The book was in fact more subversive than Montesquieu's *Persian Letters* had been, since it sang the praises of a very real neighbor, where the fruits of England's religious toleration and political liberty were to be seen both in scientific accomplishments of the English and in the commercial prosperity they enjoyed. The Parlement of Paris, France's highest court of appeals, reacted accordingly and banned the *Letters Concerning the English Nation* in 1734. Voltaire was forced to resume his wanderings, which now went on for a quarter-century. He spent most of the years 1734–43 in happy and productive cohabitation with Madame du Châtelet, a formidable Enlightenment thinker in her own right, with a cooperatively absent husband, at her estate at Cirey, in Lorraine. In addition to an unabated flow of dramas and verse, Voltaire now became the most innovative historian of the early Enlightenment. His great study of Louis XIV in fact restored him briefly to favor at Versailles, where he became historiographer to the king in 1745. Relations with Madame du Châtelet had in the meantime soured, though she and Voltaire reunited in 1749 at her deathbed, during childbirth, together with her husband and current lover. Voltaire was now banished from the capital again, and later in the same year, he finally accepted the long-standing invitation of Frederick, Prussia's energetic young king, to join the royal court at Berlin. A shorter, more intense replay of his life at Cirey ensued: an initial period of blissful productivity—Voltaire, who was probably bisexual, and Frederick, certainly homosexual, may even have been lovers for a time—was followed by a fractious blowup between the two powerful personalities. House arrest and flight back to France followed in 1753. Having failed to establish himself at two absolutist courts, Voltaire was now virtually a man without a country. He was, however, wealthy, thanks in part to his literary success but still more to his skills as financier and investor. In 1755, he leased a modest estate in the Swiss city-state of Geneva. As Voltaire remarked at the time, Les Délices (the Delights), as he called it, which he shared with his niece, Madame Denis, the other great female love of his life, was the first household that he actually headed rather than lived in as a guest.

It was at Les Délices, in 1758, that Voltaire wrote *Candide*, which was preceded by a number of earlier exercises in the genre of the "philosophical tale." He was sixty-four at the time. Surprisingly, given a lifetime of complaints about ill health, *Candide* proved not to be a swan song but instead ushered in an entirely new phase of Voltaire's life, one of even greater hyperactivity. In 1759, he purchased the more ample estates of Ferney and Tournay, just across the border from Geneva, in France. Scandalized by the dismal state of peasant life in the villages he now superintended, Voltaire threw himself into improving the local agricultural economy, with notable success. More important, it was from Ferney that he launched the great public campaigns against judicial abuse that were the hallmark of the political activity of his later years. Voltaire had in fact tried unsuccessfully some years earlier to intervene on behalf of Admiral Byng, the British naval commander shot for cowardice—the inspiration for chapter 23 of *Candide*. In 1762, Voltaire's attention was captured by the brutal public execution in Toulouse of Jean Calas, a Protestant businessman falsely accused of having murdered his son, a suicide. Voltaire devoted three years of incessant labor to clearing Calas's name, during which time he sheltered his widow and children. The Calas campaign was the first of a string of militant interventions on behalf of victims of religious persecution and social abuse, inspired by the sentiment expressed in the motto Voltaire now used to sign letters: "Ecrasez l'infâme!"—"Crush the infamy!" Voltaire's correspondence was in fact gargantuan: the evidence suggests that he may have written more than forty thousand personal letters in his lifetime, of which some fifteen thousand survive. Meanwhile, his formal literary output flagged not a bit in this period. His *Philosophical Dictionary* (1764) is a masterpiece of the mature Enlightenment. Accompanying it were any number of tales, essays, dramas, and poems, which continued to pour forth from Voltaire's pen until his last days. These were in fact spent in Paris in the first half of 1778, where Voltaire finally returned, after an absence of nearly thirty years, to attend the première of one last tragedy. There his health finally failed him, but before his death on May 30, the eighty-four-year-old writer was treated to rapturous public celebrations.

Voltaire's conquest of Paris was more than a personal victory, of course. It was the moment of greatest triumph for the Enlightenment itself, with which he had by now become so closely identified. The intimate association between writer and movement, however, poses a question about *Candide,* the greatest literary success of Voltaire's lifetime. A reader coming to the story anew might be forgiven for finding the relation between text and context puzzling—or even discrepant. For there is, of course, no idea more commonly associated with the Enlightenment, in its maturity, than a belief in "progress"—a fundamental optimism about the capacity of modern Europeans to reshape the social and political world for the better. Yet *Candide* is, of all things, a *satire* on "optimism," whose object is precisely one of those intellectual pioneers that the Enlightenment, and Voltaire in particular, tended otherwise to honor—the German philosopher Leibniz, author of the doctrine ventriloquized by Pangloss in the story. Indeed, the ordeals to which its protagonist is subject—expulsion from an Edenic home; a succession of misadventures whose hallmark is hyperbolic physical violence; and final capture of the object of his affections, only to find that he no longer desires her—seem designed to make the case for the opposite doctrine, the *pessimism* (a word Voltaire may have invented), urged by Pangloss's opposite number, Martin. In the meantime, as if to agree that this is the worst of possible worlds, the Old Woman who arrives so memorably in chapters 11 and 12 has already insisted that *every* human life is fundamentally a tale of misfortune and suffering. If we compare the outlook of *Candide* to, say, *The Marriage of Figaro,* with its triumphantly happy end, then Voltaire's story might look less like an advertisement for the Enlightenment than the announcement of his defection from it.

There were, in fact, contemporary commentators who read *Candide* that way and suggested an obvious biographical explanation for Voltaire's disenchantment. After all, the relative happiness of his life at Cirey, when he and Madame du Châtelet were indeed enthusiasts for Leibniz, ended with a series of heavy personal blows—the breakup with Châtelet and her premature death, permanent loss of favor at Versailles, the imbroglio with Frederick and expulsion from Prussia. These private tragedies were then followed, in the mid-1750s, by two major public catastrophes, which deeply engaged Voltaire's imagination—the great earthquake that destroyed Lisbon in 1755, claiming thousands of lives, and the outbreak of the Seven Years' War, strewing destruction around the globe, the following year. The earthquake was, in fact, the occasion for a famous poem, in which Voltaire explicitly attacked Leibniz. *Candide,* the argument goes, simply clinched the case against "optimism" by distilling these experiences into a thinly veiled autobiography: the sufferings of its main characters mirror those of its author all too exactly, for which the Seven Years' War (that is, the war between Bulgars and Avars in chapters 2 through 4) and the Lisbon earthquake (experienced at firsthand by Candide and Pangloss in chapter 5) furnish the appropriate historical backdrop. On this view, which has had many adherents, *Candide* was indeed out of step with the Enlightenment, a grumpy exception to its optimism and faith in progress.

However, this is not the only way to understand the relation of *Candide* to its biographical and intellectual context. The historian David Wootton has recently proposed an alternative account, arguing that the book played an even more pivotal role in Voltaire's life than has hitherto been recognized. Laying special stress on Voltaire's well-attested and frequently repeated complaints about being sexually abused by his Jesuit teachers as a child, Wootton contends that this defining experience—together with the ordeals of physical violence, imprisonment, exile, exaltation and degradation, love and loss that followed over the next forty years—did indeed supply the raw material for *Candide*. By the time he wrote it, however, Voltaire had reached the safe shore of Les Délices and was now genuinely *happy*, for perhaps the first time in his life. *Candide* is testimony to that achievement. Far from announcing an embrace of pessimism, what the story reveals is the *means* by which Voltaire freed himself from an unhappy past: he unburdened himself by finally telling his story, in precisely the manner that his main characters do. That the purge was successful, Wootton concludes, is shown by what followed in the last phase of Voltaire's life, with his turn to energetic and effective political activism.

There are limits to any biographical explanation of a work of imaginative literature, of course. But Wootton's interpretation has the advantage of explaining salient features of *Candide*, difficult to account for otherwise. First, if there is any single characteristic of *Candide* on which all readers agree, it is surely its sheer *exuberance* as a piece of writing—a bubbling gaiety of form, belying its apparently grim contents, that accords perfectly with Voltaire's frequent descriptions of his newfound happiness in his correspondence of the time. As for those contents, the basic component part of the story is, of course, the slip on the banana peel—the sudden dashing of hopes, reversal of fortune, puncturing of illusions. The constant repetition of this joke, in myriad forms, is, in fact, what supplies the basic evidence for the "pessimistic" reading of *Candide*. However, once larger narrative patterns come into sight—above all with the numerous "stories-within-the-story," as new characters appear or old ones reappear—a more complicated picture emerges. For these narratives all focus obsessively on precisely the topic indicated by Wootton's interpretation—sexuality, and sexual violence in particular. Violation at the hands of men is the fate of every female character in *Candide*, suffering as a result of their own sexual sins the lot of all the men. This is true for the protagonist no less than for the rest: Candide is exiled from a happy home for a sexual slip, and his dogged pursuit of his lost love object across three continents ends in what might be thought of as the bitterest ironic reversal of all.

That the ending of *Candide* is not at all bitter, however, is owing to its *other* narrative thread, which more than compensates for this bleak depiction of sexuality and erotic love. *Candide* opens with a depiction of a community that is an elfin model of Old Regime European society as a whole—hierarchical, authoritarian, laughably unaware of its own poverty, convinced that it is the best of possible worlds. In fact, the smallest sexual indiscretion is enough to unravel Thunder-ten-Tronckh, flinging its inhabitants out into a world of violence and misfortune. Halfway through his journey toward a new home, however, Candide stumbles on a second community, Eldorado, which is the exact opposite of the first—"enlightened," egalitarian, blissfully unaware of its own wealth, oblivious to the fact that it *is* the best of possible worlds. But Candide learns its lessons and departs a wealthy man. By the end of the story, he has forged a new community out of the debris of the first one, replacing the Baron (old and young) at the head of a society that is egalitarian, wealthy enough to be well fed, and undeluded about its place in the cosmos. For if the ridiculous "optimism" of Pangloss is indeed formally abandoned, immediately on leaving Eldorado, Candide does not thereby embrace the equally absurd "pessimism" advocated by Martin. Philosophically, the last word belongs to the dervish of chapter 30, who literally slams the door on dogmatic speculative philosophy of every kind. Far more convincing than any speculative system is the concluding example of the old farmer, who, more contented than any king in Europe, demonstrates that happiness is well within reach, to be secured by pulling together and *working* at it.

From Thunder-ten-Tronckh via Eldorado to the farm outside Constantinople—an itinerary perhaps not all that far from *The Marriage of Figaro* after all. What this suggests, at the least, is that posterity has made no mistake in regarding *Candide* as the best of all possible renderings of Enlightenment ideas in literary form. Trying to explain the unique place of Shakespeare in English literature, the poet Ted Hughes once suggested that "it is only those poets whose make-up somehow coincides with the vital impulse of their times who are able to come to real stature." Voltaire is a lesser writer, of course, but there was clearly a happy coincidence between the biographical material that found expression in *Candide* and the "vital impulse" of his time. The result was a winning allegory of the process of enlightenment itself, as Candide's journey through the European world gradually causes the dogmatic scales to fall from his eyes. Along the way, the reader is treated to the entire catalogue of great Enlightenment themes—condensed into the charming mini-utopia of Eldorado but, above all, leaping out from Voltaire's scathing description of the injustice, irrationality, and violence of European society, metropolitan and colonial, in the rest of the text. For all of Voltaire's circumspection in dealing with the various kings who cross his pages—objects of pathos as much as ridicule—the silhouette of a revolutionary politics is not hard to glimpse in *Candide*. Shortly after its initial publication, the American and French Revolutions in fact started start the process of dismantling the social world of aristocrats and kings that we now call the Old Regime. What is striking, two and a half centuries later, is not merely how violent that undertaking turned out to be but also how slowly it has proceeded. This is true for the world of thought as well—which, of course, is precisely why *Candide*'s satire has remained so actual, and so entertaining, over the years. Despite the efforts of Voltaire, his fellow Enlightenment thinkers, and their successors, our own intellectual scene teems with Panglosses and Martins, peddling prefabricated systems of thought of every kind. The consolations of facile "optimism" and "pessimism" alike are as attractive as ever. But so long as this is the case, *Candide* is not likely to lack for readers.

Translator's Note

Voltaire is a master satirist, often skewering targets with a rapier in each hand. His mind is so full, his verbal celerity so dazzling, that the narrative drive, the force and pace of *Candide* have made it compulsory reading for two hundred and fifty years. Nor do readers soon forget its lessons, any more than they do its wit or the resplendently visualized characters who spin in the plot's rapidly moving wheels.

This is not the satire of *The Dunciad*, Alexander Pope's overfreighted, now almost unreadable mock epic. Voltaire builds his story out of material current in 1759 but manages to find what is universal without insisting on what is long dead and forgotten. Candide, Pangloss, Cunégonde, and the other denizens of his flashing world would need only a change of costume to walk the streets of New York or San Francisco. Their problems may stem from particularities we no longer fully share, but the *reasons* that underlie them, and the *effects* they have, remain instantly recognizable.

Despite the book's age, accordingly, there is no need to footnote its references or to explain its exact allusions, except in the few and unusual instances when comprehension becomes difficult—or impossible—if the reader is not offered a small helping hand. To refer to a man who has *epousé sa commère* ("married the godchild of his godmother") as simply *un Biscayen,* as Voltaire does, conveys no more of what is intended than the reference that follows hard on its heels, toward the end of chapter 5, to *deux Portugais qui en mangeant un poulet en avaient arraché le lard.* Any good English-language dictionary can explain that the Bay of Biscay is on the north and the west of Spain. The information seems irrelevant, though in 1759 it was not. And modern readers are basically bewildered by "two Portuguese who, when eating a chicken, removed the bacon." In the first case, I have referred to the helpless innocent in question as a man from the northern mountains of Spain—that is, a rural innocent, likely to be unlearned in the finer points of canon or any other kind of law. And to explain the chicken eaters adequately, I have added to Voltaire's text that the two Portuguese were suspected of acting as Jews—that is, carefully not eating bacon—though they were officially Catholic.

In short, though both my rule and my inclination are to translate as close to the original French as I can, and for the most part I have done only and exactly that, there are occasional exceptions. These are neither embroidery nor frivolities but examples of how a two-hundred-and-fifty-year-old text can force translators into a corner, from which they escape only by resorting to literary legerdemain. I have even been driven, at a grand total of six places, to the despairing use of footnotes, albeit exceedingly brief ones.

Note that in Voltaire's day the French word *jardin* meant "fields" or a place where one cultivated either medicinal plants or assorted vegetation from around the world. Indeed, until the nineteenth century the English word "garden" had the same meaning; the adjectives "flower" or "private" were still required to indicate the newer and now prevalent meaning. At the end of *Candide* the word Voltaire uses, *jardin*, has been regularly mistranslated (for our time) as "garden."

This translation is based on the Pléiade edition, edited by Frédéric Deloffre (Paris: Gallimard, 1979).

Candide

Chapter One

How Candide was raised in a noble mansion, and how he was driven away

In Westphalia, in Baron Thunder-den-tronckh's mansion, lived a young man born wonderfully mild and gentle. His face revealed his soul. He possessed a sufficiency of good sense, and a profoundly straightforward mind—which is why, I believe, he'd been named Candide. The old household servants suspected he was son to the Baron's sister and a good, respectable gentleman who lived nearby, with whom the lady refused to be married, since he could only prove seventy-one percent of his ancestry, the remainder of his genealogical tree having been destroyed by the ravages of time.

The Baron was one of Westphalia's most potent aristocrats, since his mansion boasted both a door and windows. His great dining hall was even hung with a tapestry. All the barnyard dogs served, when required, as a pack of hunting hounds; his stable hands beat the bushes for birds; the village priest was his household chaplain. Everyone called him My Lord, and they laughed when he told stories.

The Baroness, weighing close to three hundred pounds, attracted a good deal of attention, and was such a dignified hostess that her reputation swelled still further. Her daughter, Cunégonde, was seventeen, rosy-faced, glowing, plump, tempting. The Baron's son seemed entirely worthy of his father. Their tutor, Pangloss, was the household oracle, and little Candide listened to him with all the good faith of youth and his own sweet disposition.

What Pangloss taught was metaphysico-theologico-cosmonigology. He demonstrated perfectly that there was no effect without a cause and that, in this best of all possible worlds, the Baron's mansion was the most beautiful of all mansions and the Baroness the best of all possible baronesses.

"Manifestly," he said, "nothing could have been different. Since everything was designed for a purpose, everything is necessarily meant to serve the best of all purposes. Observe how noses are designed to hold up eyeglasses, and therefore we have eyeglasses. Legs are obviously meant for wearing shoes, and so we have shoes. Rocks having been designed to be quarried and used for building purposes, the Baron has a singularly beautiful mansion. The greatest Baron in Westphalia requires the greatest dwelling—and because pigs were made to be eaten, we dine on pork all year long. Accordingly, those who have suggested that everything is good have spoken obtusely: what they should have said is that everything is for the best."

Candide listened very carefully, and believed with utter innocence, because he found Miss Cunégonde extraordinarily beautiful, though he never had the nerve to tell her so. To be born Baron of Thunder-den-tronckh, he had concluded, was the greatest happiness of all, but the second level of happiness was to be Miss Cunégonde, and the third was to see her every day, and the fourth was to listen to Maître Pangloss, the greatest philosopher in Westphalia and therefore in the whole world.

One day, while walking outside the mansion, in the little wood they called their "estate," Cunégonde saw that, in the bushes, Dr. Pangloss was giving practical lessons in natural science to her mother's chambermaid, a petite, very pretty and compliant brunette. Because Miss Cunégonde was immensely interested in matters scientific, she took careful notice, not so much as breathing, of the repeated experimental truths she was witnessing. She saw very clearly the doctor's satisfactory purpose, both its intentions and its results, and then she went away highly restless and unsettled, deeply thoughtful, filled with a desire to study these matters herself, imagining that she might very well be a satisfactory purpose for young Candide, who could likewise serve in that capacity for her.

On the way back to the mansion, she met Candide, and blushed. Candide blushed, too. She said "Hello," her voice trembling, and Candide talked to her without knowing what he was saying. The next day, after dinner, when they had left the table, Cunégonde and Candide found themselves behind a folding screen. Cunégonde dropped her handkerchief, Candide picked it up, she quite innocently grasped his hand, and the young man quite innocently kissed hers, with his completely distinctive grace, liveliness, and sensitivity. Their lips met, their eyes burned, their knees shook, their hands wandered. Baron Thunder-den-tronckh, passing by, saw this cause and this effect, and immediately drove Candide from the house, kicking violently at the boy's backside. Cunégonde fainted; the Baroness slapped her in the face, the moment the girl came to herself; and then everything was topsy-turvy in the most beautiful, the most charming of all possible mansions.

Chapter Two

What happened to Candide among the Bulgars

Driven out of this earthly paradise, Candide walked for a long time, not knowing where he was going, weeping, raising his eyes to heaven, and constantly looking back toward the noblest of mansions, containing the most beautiful of all baronial daughters. He lay down, hungry, out in the fields, between two furrows. Fat snowflakes fell.

The next day, frozen stiff, Candide dragged himself to the nearby village, called Valdberghoff-trarbk-dikdorff, without a penny in his pocket, dying of hunger and weariness. He stopped, sorrowfully, at the door of an inn. Two men dressed in blue noticed him.

"Comrade," said one, "there's a young fellow, well built, and exactly the right height."

They approached Candide and, most politely, invited him to have dinner with them.

"Gentlemen," replied Candide, charmingly straightforward, "you much honor me, but I have nothing with which to pay my share."

"Ah, sir!" one of the blue coats told him, "worthy people with a face like yours never need to pay a cent. Aren't you five feet, five inches tall?"

"Yes, gentlemen. That is exactly my height," he said, bowing.

"Ah, sir! Come and sit down. Not only will we pay your share, but we wouldn't ever allow a man like you to walk with an empty purse. Men aren't meant to turn their backs on one another."

"That's right," said Candide. "That's exactly what Maître Pangloss always told me, and I can see quite clearly that everything is indeed for the best."

They pressed several shillings on him, which he took and for which he tried to give them a promissory note. They refused anything of the sort and led him to the table.

"Aren't you a devoted lover?"

"Oh yes," he answered. "I love Miss Cunégonde most devotedly."

"No," said one of these gentlemen. "What we're asking is whether you're devoted to the King of the Bulgars."

"Not at all," he said, "because I've never seen him."

"What! He's the most delightful of all kings, and we must drink his health."

"Oh, most willingly, gentlemen."

And so he drank.

"That will do it," one of them told him. "Now you're the upholder, sustainer, defender, and hero of everything Bulgar. Your fortune is made, your fame is assured."

They promptly put him in leg irons and led him to his regiment. He was obliged to turn right, turn left, pick up his musket, put down his musket, aim his musket, fire it, march very rapidly, and then they struck him thirty times with a stick. The next day he performed the drill a bit less badly, and they hit him only twenty times. The day after that he got only ten blows, and his comrades considered him a prodigy.

Completely stunned, Candide couldn't quite figure out how he'd become a hero. One fine spring day, he felt like going for a walk, following his nose in a straight line, for it seemed to him an inherent right of all human beings, like all animals, to use their limbs as they pleased. He hadn't gone five miles when, suddenly, four other heroes, six feet tall, overtook him, tied him up, and led him to jail. Following the letter of the law, he was permitted to choose whether he preferred being beaten thirty-six times by each man in the regiment or being shot in the head by a volley of twelve lead bullets. He was informed that the decision was entirely up to him, and even though he replied that men enjoyed freedom of the will and he preferred neither one nor the other, he was still required to make a choice. He decided, considering God's great gift of "liberty," to run the gauntlet thirty-six times. He managed it twice. There were two thousand men in the regiment, which resulted in four thousand blows and, from neck to ass hole, the exposure of his muscles and nerves. As they were about to proceed with the third round, Candide was incapable of any more and asked if, as a great favor, they would mind blowing out his brains. They granted his request; he was blindfolded, they made him kneel.

At that moment, the Bulgar King came by, and inquired into the condemned man's crime. Being a man of immense intellect, the King understood, from what they told him, that Candide was a youthful metaphysician, utterly ignorant of worldly matters, and from the goodness of his heart pardoned the young man, for which he will be praised in every newspaper and across all the ages. A fine physician cured Candide in three weeks, using unguents first prescribed by that wild ancient Greek Dioscorides. Candide had already grown back some of his skin, and was able to walk, when the Bulgar King declared war on the Scythian Abars.

Chapter Three

How Candide saved himself from the Bulgars, and what became of him

Nothing was ever so fine, so elegant, so gleamingly brilliant, so well-ordered as the two armies. Their trumpets, flutes, oboes, drums, and cannon created harmonies only ever heard in hell. First the cannon blew away almost six thousand men on each side, and then rifle fire removed from this best of all worlds some roughly nine to ten thousand wretches who'd been infecting its surface. Bayonets became a satisfactory cause of death for some thousands more. The total came to perhaps thirty thousand souls. Candide, shaking like a philosopher, hid himself as well as he could during this heroic butchery.

Finally, as the two kings ordered that a *Te Deum* be sung, each in his own camp, Candide decided to go somewhere else in order to analyze causes and effects. Climbing over heaps of dead and dying, he reached a neighboring village that had been reduced to ashes. This was an Abar village, burned by the Bulgars according to the rules of international law. Here old men beaten black and blue had watched their slaughtered wives die, holding babies to their bloody breasts. There disemboweled girls, having first satisfied the natural needs of numbers of heroes, had shuddered their final breath, and others, half burned, had screamed for someone to come and kill them. Brains were scattered all over the ground, along with severed arms and legs.

Candide ran even faster to another village, belonging to the Bulgars and to which heroic Abars had given the same treatment. Constantly stepping on twitching limbs or over ruins, Candide finally put the battlefields behind him, carrying a bit of food in his knapsack and never forgetting Miss Cunégonde. By the time he got to Holland he had no food left, but having heard it said that everyone in this country was rich, and was also Christian, he hadn't the slightest doubt of receiving the same treatment as, once, he'd known in the Baron's great mansion, before Miss Cunégonde's beautiful eyes had caused him to be driven away.

He begged alms of several sober persons, each of whom told him that, if he continued to practice this profession, they'd have him locked away in a house of correction, where he would be taught how to live.

The next person to whom he applied was a man who, for a solid hour, alone and unaided, had been talking to a large audience about charity. Scowling at Candide, the orator said:

"Why are you here? Have you come for the Grand Cause?"

"There is no effect without a cause," Candide replied, simply. "Everything is linked together and designed for the best. I had to be driven away from Miss Cunégonde, and I had to run the gauntlet, and I have to beg for my bread until I'm able to earn it. Nothing could have been different."

"My friend," said the orator, "do you believe the Pope is Antichrist?"

"I've never heard anyone say so," answered Candide. "But whether he is or he isn't, I have nothing to eat."

"You don't deserve to eat," said the other man. "Get out of here, rascal—leave me alone, wretch—if you want to stay alive, keep away from me."

The orator's wife, who came to a window and heard a man doubting the Pope was Antichrist, poured out on his head a full . . . O heaven! How women are carried away by religious zeal!

A man who had never been baptized, a good Anabaptist named Jacques, saw the cruel and humiliating way they were treating one his brothers, a being with two feet and quite without feathers, a being who had a soul, and brought him to his own home, washed him, gave him bread and beer and a gift of two gold florins, and even offered to teach him how to make Persian fabrics, as they were manufactured in Holland. Candide came close to falling at his feet.

"Maître Pangloss was absolutely right, saying that everything is for the best in this world, because I'm infinitely more moved by your extraordinary generosity than by the harshness of that man in the black coat and his wife."

Taking a walk, the next day, he met a beggar covered with pus-filled sores, his eyes blank, the tip of his nose rotted away, his mouth twisted, his teeth black, speaking from deep in his throat, racked by a violent cough, and spitting out a tooth with every word.

Chapter Four

How Candide met his old philosophy teacher, Doctor Pangloss, and what had happened to him

Stirred more by pity than by horror, Candide gave this ghastly beggar the two gold pieces he'd received from his honest Anabaptist, Jacques. The specter stared at him, shed a few tears, and flung his arms around Candide's neck. Frightened, Candide backed away.

"Alas!" cried one wretch to the other. "Don't you recognize your beloved Pangloss?"

"What? You, my dear teacher! You, in that horrible condition! What misfortune could have fallen on you? Why aren't you still living in the loveliest of all mansions? What's become of Miss Cunégonde, gem of all women, nature's masterpiece?"

"I can't go on," said Pangloss.

Once he'd been brought to the Anabaptist's stable, where he

managed to eat a bit of bread and his strength was renewed, Candide asked:

"Well now! What about Cunégonde?"

"She's dead," he was told.

Hearing this, Candide fainted. Pangloss revived him with a bit of spoiled vinegar that, by pure chance, he found in the stable. Candide opened his eyes.

"Cunégonde dead! Best of all possible worlds, where have you gone? But what sickness killed her? Surely, it wasn't because she saw me being kicked in the backside and driven from her father's fine mansion?"

"No," said Pangloss. "She'd been disemboweled by Bulgar soldiers, after she'd been raped as many times as conceivably possible. They smashed in the Baron's head, because he tried to defend her; the Baroness was chopped into little pieces; my poor pupil, her brother, was treated exactly like his sister; and as for the mansion, there isn't a single stone left—not a barn, not a single sheep, not a duck, not a tree. But we were well avenged, because the Abars did the same thing to a neighboring baron, who was a Bulgar."

Hearing this, Candide fainted again, but recovered unaided, and having said what it was right and necessary to say, he inquired about the cause and effect, and the satisfactory purpose, that had brought Pangloss to so pitiful a state.

"Alas!" said he. "It was love—love, comforter of the human species, guardian of the universe, soul of every feeling creature—love, tender love."

"Alas!" said Candide. "I've known it, this love, this lord of all hearts, this soul of our souls. All it's been worth to me is a kiss and twenty kicks in the backside. How could so beautiful a cause create, in you, such an abominable effect?"

Pangloss replied as follows:

"O my dear Candide! You've met Paquette, our noble Baroness's pretty servant. In her arms I've tasted the delights of paradise, and that's what brought me the hellish suffering you see eating me alive. She'd been infected by it; perhaps she even died of it. She'd received this gift from a learned Franciscan friar, who had traced it back to its source: he had gotten it from an old countess, who had gotten it from a captain in the cavalry, who had gotten it from a marquise, who had gotten it from her young servant, who had gotten it from a Jesuit, who, as a novice, had gotten it in a straight line from one of Christopher Columbus's comrades. Me, I haven't given it to anyone, because I'm dying of it."

"O Pangloss!" cried Candide. "What a strange genealogy! Surely the devil spawned it?"

"Not at all," replied the great philosopher. "It was absolutely necessary, in this best of all worlds, a vital ingredient, because if Columbus hadn't picked it up, on some island in the Americas—this affliction that poisons the organ of human procreation, which has even completely prevented procreation, and is plainly directly contrary to the fundamental purposes of nature—we would never have had either chocolate or cochineal dye. It's important to note that, even today, the affliction is distinctly European, like religious controversy. Turks, Indians, Persians, Chinese, Siamese, Japanese still have no acquaintance with it, though there is a satisfactory reason why, in a few centuries, they, too, will have their turn. In the meantime, the disease has made wonderful progress among us, especially in the massive armies of respectable, well-bred mercenaries, who decide the destiny of nations. One can comfortably assume that when thirty thousand men fight a battle with a force of the same number, there will be twenty thousand cases of syphilis on each side."

"Remarkable," said Candide. "But we've got to cure you."

"And how?" said Pangloss. "I haven't got a penny, my friend, and nowhere across the whole globe can you get your stomach purged or have an enema without paying, or having someone else pay for you."

For Candide, these words settled the matter. He went and threw himself at the feet of Jacques, his charitable Anabaptist, and gave him so moving an account of the state to which his old friend had been reduced that the good man at once took in Doctor Pangloss and had him cured at his own expense. While he was being cured, Pangloss lost only one ear and one eye. And since he wrote a fine hand, and knew arithmetic perfectly, Jacques made him his bookkeeper.

Two months later, his business requiring a trip to Lisbon, he embarked on his own ship, taking the two philosophers with him. Pangloss explained to him how everything was always for the best. Jacques did not think so.

"Of course," he said, "men must have corrupted nature, since they were surely not born wolves, and wolves is what they've become. God gave them neither huge cannons nor bayonets, and they've made cannons and bayonets for their own destruction. I might say the same thing of bankruptcy, and the law that snatches up a bankrupt's property, in order to cheat his creditors."

"All absolutely essential," answered the one-eyed doctor. "These individual misfortunes are for the general good: the more individual misfortunes there are, the more everything is as it ought to be."

As he was arguing, the sky darkened, winds blew up from the four corners of the earth, and as the port of Lisbon came into view, the ship was caught in a truly horrible storm.

Chapter Five

Tempest, shipwreck, earthquake, and what happened to
Doctor Pangloss, Candide, and Jacques the Anabaptist

Half the passengers, sickened and weak, close to death from the incredible suffering caused by a ship's wild rolling, their nerves and all their senses pulled first one way and then another, were quite unable to worry about danger. The other half screamed and said prayers. The sails were stripped away, the masts snapped, the ship was breaking apart. Those who were still able to, worked; none of them knew what they were doing; no one was in charge.

The Anabaptist was doing what he could to help, standing on the main deck, when a raging sailor hit him so hard he was stretched out on the deck, but the shock of such a violent blow sent the sailor himself headfirst off the ship. He hung there, suspended from part of a broken mast. Worthy Jacques ran to his aid, helped him climb back up, and in the process was thrown into the sea, in full sight of the sailor, who let him sink, not troubling even to watch. Candide came over and saw his benefactor come up one last time, then disappear forever. He tried to throw himself into the sea, but philosopher Pangloss held him back, demonstrating that Lisbon harbor had been created expressly so that the Anabaptist could drown in it. While he was proving this, a priori, the ship split apart and everyone died except Pangloss, Candide, and the savage sailor who had caused the Anabaptist's death: the scoundrel was lucky enough to swim to shore, to which Pangloss and Candide were carried on a plank.

When they'd more or less recovered, they walked toward Lisbon. They still had a bit of money, with which they hoped, having escaped the storm, to save themselves from starvation.

Hardly had they set foot in the city, still weeping for the death of their benefactor, when they felt the earth shaking under their feet. The sea boiled and swirled, smashing every ship anchored in the harbor. Fire blew up in whirlwinds, ashes and cinders covered streets and public places; houses collapsed, roofs flattened down to foundations, and foundations smashed and were scattered. Thirty thousand people, of both sexes and of all ages, lay crushed in the ruins. The sailor whistled, and swore:

"A man might make a bit of money, here."

"What could be the satisfactory purpose of such a phenomenon?" said Pangloss.

"This is the end of the world!" cried Candide.

The sailor dashed right into the debris, challenging death so he could find gold, and found it, and took it, then drank himself drunk, and when he'd slept it off, bought himself the first willing woman he met with, among the ruins of destroyed houses and in the middle of the dead and dying.

But Pangloss took hold of his sleeve.

"My friend," he said, "this isn't right. You're defying universal reason, you've misunderstood what's going on here."

"God damn it to hell!" said the sailor. "I'm a sailor, I was born in Batavia, I've spat on the crucifix four times, so I could get myself into Japan! You've found the right man, you and your universal reason!"

A shower of stones hit Candide; he lay in the street, covered with dirt and dust. He said to Pangloss:

"Help! Bring me a little wine and some oil. I'm dying."

"Earthquakes are nothing new," replied Pangloss. "Last year, in the Americas, Lima experienced the same thing—the same causes, the same effects. There's definitely a vein of sulfur running underground, from Lima to Lisbon."

"Nothing is more likely," said Candide. "But for the love of God, get me a little oil and some wine."

"What do you mean, likely?" the philosopher answered. "I'd argue that the thing has been proven."

Candide lost consciousness, and Pangloss brought him a bit of water from a nearby fountain.

The next day, having found a bit of food as they groped through the rubble, they managed to resuscitate themselves. And then, as others were doing, they helped dig out those who'd escaped death. Sometimes, people they'd personally saved offered them as good a dinner as possible, in such a scene of disaster. Naturally, it was a sad meal, the survivors weeping as they ate, but Pangloss assured them that things could not possibly have been different:

"Because," he said, "this is all for the best. Because, if there's a volcano in Lisbon, it couldn't be anywhere else. Because it's impossible that things would not be as they in fact are. Because everything is for the best."

A dark-skinned little man, sitting alongside, who was intimately acquainted with the Inquisition, spoke up, most politely:

"Apparently the gentleman is not a believer in original sin, since if everything is indeed for the best, there could neither have been a fall nor any punishment on that account."

"I most humbly beg Your Excellency's pardon," said Pangloss even more politely, "since the fall of man and the resulting curse are necessary components of the best of all possible worlds."

"Does the gentleman not believe in freedom of the will?"

"Do please excuse me, Your Excellency," said Pangloss. "Freedom of the will can certainly co-exist with absolute necessity, because it was necessary that we be this free, because, in short, predestination . . . ."

Pangloss was in the middle of these remarks when the dark-skinned little man gave a signal, by a movement of his head, to the attendant who was pouring him a glass of port, also known as wine from Oporto.

Chapter Six

How they had a beautiful auto-da-fé in order to put an end to the earthquake, and how Candide was flogged

After the earthquake, which had destroyed three quarters of Lisbon, the country's wise men could find no better way of preventing total ruin than to give the people a beautiful auto-da-fé. It was decided, by Coimbra University, that the sight of people being burned alive over a slow fire, and very ceremoniously, was nature's infallible, mysterious method of keeping the earth from shaking.

Accordingly, they had rounded up a man from Spain's northern mountains, convicted of having married his godchild's godmother, and two Portuguese who, dining on a chicken roasted with bacon, had removed the bacon before eating, thus proving themselves secret Jews. And after the friendly dinner, they came and tied up Doctor Pangloss and his disciple, Candide, the one for having spoken and the other for having listened, looking as if he approved. Both were locked up, separately, in extremely cold quarters where there was no need to worry about the sun shining. Eight days later, both were dressed in the yellow robes of condemned heretics, and their heads were adorned with paper caps. Candide's robe and cap were painted with upside-down flames and devils without either tails or claws, but Pangloss's devils had both tails and claws and the flames burned straight up. Thus attired, they marched in a procession, and listened to an infinitely pathetic sermon, followed by beautiful music, sung in harmonious contrapuntal style. Candide was flogged in time with the music; the two men who refused to eat bacon, and the Spanish mountain dweller, were burned alive; and Pangloss was hanged, though that was not the usual procedure. That very day the earth shook once more, producing frightful groaning and roaring.

Candide, horror-stricken, dumbfounded, overcome, covered with blood and shaking, said to himself:

"If this is the best of all possible worlds, what are the others like? But still, if I hadn't been flogged, I'd still be with the Bulgars. But O, my dear Pangloss! Greatest of all philosophers, did I have to see you hanged, not knowing why! O my dear Anabaptist, the best of men, did you have to be drowned in the harbor! O Miss Cunégonde! Jewel of women, did you have to have your belly slit open!"

He was coming back to himself, just barely able to function, having been preached at, flogged, absolved, and blessed, when an old woman came over and said:

"Lift up your heart, my son, and follow me."

Chapter Seven

How an old woman took care of Candide and how he got
back his beloved

Candide's heart was not uplifted, but he followed the old woman
into a dirty shack. She gave him a jar of ointment to rub on his back
and left him food and drink. She showed him a small bed, quite
decent, next to which there was a complete set of clothes.

"Eat, drink, sleep," she told him. "And may Our Lady of Atocha,
and Saint Anthony of Padua, and Saint James of Compostela watch
over you. I'll come back tomorrow."

Still stunned by everything he had seen, everything he had suffered, and even more by the old woman's kind charity, Candide tried
to kiss her hand.

"Mine isn't the hand you ought to be kissing," she said. "I'll come
back tomorrow. Rub yourself with ointment, eat, and sleep."

In spite of all the misery he had experienced, Candide ate
and slept. The next day the old woman brought him breakfast, in-
spected his back, and rubbed it herself, with a different ointment.
Later in the day she brought him dinner, then returned at night and
brought him supper. The day afterward she performed the same
ceremonies.

"Who are you?" Candide kept asking her. "What inspires you to
such kindness? What could I possibly do for you?"

The good woman never answered, but that night, when she returned, she did not bring him any supper.

"Come with me," she said, "and don't say a word."

She took him by the arm and they walked perhaps a quarter of a mile into the countryside. They came to a house that had no other dwellings nearby; it was encircled by gardens and drainage ditches. The old woman knocked at a small door. It was opened; she led Candide to a hidden staircase and then into a small private room, its walls gilded, and left him on a brocade sofa, closed the door behind her, and disappeared. To Candide, it seemed completely dreamlike; he saw his entire life as a disastrous dream, and the immediate present as a pleasant one.

The old woman soon returned, supporting, with difficulty, a quivering woman with a majestic figure, gleaming with jewels and wearing a veil.

"Lift the veil," the old woman instructed Candide.

The young man approached; with a timid hand he lifted the veil. What a moment! What a surprise! He thought he was seeing Miss Cunégonde, and in fact he was, it was indeed her. His strength left him, he couldn't utter a word, and fell at her feet. Cunégonde collapsed on the sofa. The old woman showered them both with aromatic spirits; they recovered, they spoke to each other—at first in broken words, with questions and answers, with sighs, tears, and exclamations. The old woman suggested they make less noise, and left them alone.

"Ah! It's you," said Candide. "You're alive. I've found you again, here in Portugal. Were you never raped? They never split open your belly, as our philosophic Pangloss told me they had?"

"It happened," said lovely Cunégonde. "But one doesn't always die of those two misfortunes."

"But your father and mother were killed?"

"That's all too terribly true," said Cunégonde, weeping.

"And your brother?"

"My brother, too, was killed."

"And why are you in Portugal? And how did you know I was here? And under what strange circumstances have you had me brought to this house?"

"I'll tell you the whole story," said the lady. "But first you have to tell me everything that happened to you, after the innocent kiss you gave me, and the kicks on the backside that you received."

With profound respect, Candide obeyed, and though he was still stunned, and his voice was shaky and weak, and his back and his ribs hurt, he told her in the simplest, most straightforward way all that had befallen him since the instant they'd been separated. Cunégonde raised her eyes to the heavens; she wept at the deaths of the good Anabaptist and Pangloss; and afterward she spoke to him as follows, not a word escaping him, as he sat and devoured her with his eyes.

Chapter Eight
Cunégonde's story

"I was in bed, in a deep sleep, when it pleased heaven to send Bulgars to our beautiful mansion, Thunder-den-tronckh. They slit my father's throat, and my brother's, and chopped my mother to bits. A big Bulgar, six feet tall, who'd seen how this spectacle made me faint away, started to rape me. That woke me up, I came to my senses, I screamed, I struggled, I bit, I scratched, I tried to rip out the big Bulgar's eyes, not understanding that everything going on in my father's mansion was a matter of custom and habit. The brute stabbed me in the left side, and I still have the scar."

"Alas! I'd love to see it," said naive Candide.

"You will see it," said Cunégonde. "But shall I go on?"

"Go on," said Candide.

And she picked up the thread of her tale, as follows:

"A Bulgar captain came in, and saw me all bloody, and how the soldier wasn't concerned at his presence. Angered by having a mere soldier show him such a lack of respect, the captain killed the soldier right on my body. Then he had my wounds treated and led me to his quarters as a prisoner of war. I washed the few shirts he had, I cooked for him. He thought me very pretty, I have to admit it, and I won't deny he wasn't badly put together, his skin was soft and white, although he didn't have much of a mind, and very little philosophy. It wasn't hard to see he hadn't been brought up by Doctor Pangloss.

"After three months, having lost all his money and grown bored with me, he sold me to a Jew named Don Issacar, who did business in Holland and Portugal and was passionately fond of women. He wanted me very badly, but he couldn't get me: I was better able to re-sist him than I'd been with the Bulgar soldier. An honorable woman may be raped once, but then her virtue grows stronger. Trying to tame me, he brought me to this country house, which you have seen. I'd always believed there was nothing on earth so lovely as Thunder-den-tronckh. This house opened my eyes.

"One day, the Grand Inquisitor noticed me at Mass, and kept looking at me; then he sent word that he had to speak to me on confidential matters. I was brought to his palace; I told him I was a baron's daughter; he explained that it was beneath my rank to belong to an Israelite. It was suggested to Don Issacar, on the Inquisitor's behalf, that he ought to sell me. Don Issacar, banker to the court and a man of great resources, wanted nothing to do with this plan. The Inquisitor threatened him with an auto-da-fé. But at last, intimidated, my Jew arranged a transaction, according to which the house and I belonged to the two of them in common. The Jew would have the right to Monday, Wednesday, and the Sabbath, and the other days of the week would belong to the Inquisitor. This arrangement has been in force for six months. It has not been free of quarrels, since it's often been unclear whether the night from Saturday to Sunday comes under the old law or the new. As for me, I've not been conquered by either one of them, and I believe that's why I've remained beloved by both.

"At last, trying to turn away the continuing plague of earthquakes, and also to intimidate Don Issacar, the Inquisitor decided to celebrate an auto-da-fé. He honored me with an invitation. I was seated most advantageously; between the Mass and the execution they served refreshments to the ladies. I was truly horrified, seeing the two Jews burned, along with that perfectly decent Spaniard who'd married his godchild's godmother, but imagine my surprise, my fright, my confusion, and my concern, when I saw, in heretic's robes and wearing a paper cap, a face that looked very like that of Pangloss! I rubbed my eyes, I watched carefully, I saw him hanged, and then I lost consciousness. I'd barely recovered my senses when I saw you stripped naked: this was the height of horror, confusion, sorrow, and despair. I can tell you, truthfully, that your skin remains whiter, and of a rosier pink hue, than my Bulgar captain's. That sight redoubled every emotion that had overwhelmed me, that had devoured me. I screamed, I wanted to say: 'Stop, barbarians!' But my voice failed me, and my cries would have been useless. When you'd been most thoroughly flogged, I said to myself: 'How can it be possible that sweet Candide and wise Pangloss find themselves in Lisbon, one to receive a hundred blows of a whip, and the other to be hanged, by order of the Inquisitor, of whom I am beloved? Pangloss has cruelly deceived me, claiming that everything is always for the best.'

"Shaken, frantic, even beside myself and ready to die of weakness, my head whirled with thoughts of my father being massacred, my mother, my brother, of that contemptuous ruffian of a Bulgar soldier and how he had stabbed me, of being enslaved, of becoming a cook and a household servant, of my Bulgar captain, of scandalous old Don Issacar, of my horrible Inquisitor, of Doctor Pangloss being hanged, of the magnificent *miserere* sung in such harmonious counterpoint while they were flogging you, and above all of the kiss I'd given you, behind the folding screen, that day when I saw you for the last time. I gave thanks to God, who had led you to me, through so many ordeals. I told my old woman to take care of you and to lead you here as soon as she could. She did exactly as I'd asked; I've had the inexpressible pleasure of seeing you once again, of listening to you, of speaking to you.

"You must be famished. I'm very, very hungry. Let's begin by eating supper."

They seated themselves at table, and after eating they went back to the fine sofa, mentioned earlier. They were there when Don Issacar, one of the house's two owners, arrived. It was the day of Sabbath. He had come to assert his legal rights, and to declare his tender love.

Chapter Nine

What happened to Cunégonde, to Candide, to the Grand Inquisitor, and to a Jew

This Issacar had the worst temper of any Hebrew seen in Israel since the Babylonian captivity.

"What!" he said. "You Christian bitch—the Inquisitor isn't enough for you? You're determined to let this rascal, too, have a share?"

And as he spoke he drew the long dagger he always wore, and believing the adverse party was unarmed, he dashed at Candide. But the old woman had given our good Westphalian, along with his new set of clothes, a first-class sword. He was the mildest and gentlest of men, but he drew his sword and laid the Israelite stone-cold dead on the floor, at lovely Cunégonde's feet.

"Mother of God!" she cried. "What will happen to us? A man killed in my own house! If the police come, we're lost."

"If Pangloss hadn't been hanged," said Candide, "he'd have given us excellent advice in this dire extremity, because he was a great philosopher. Not having him, let's consult your old woman."

The sensible old woman had started to tell them what to do when a different small door was opened. It was exactly one hour after midnight; Sunday had therefore begun. And this day was the Inquisitor's. He came in and saw Candide, so recently flogged, sword in hand, a corpse lying on the floor, Cunégonde frightened, and the old woman giving instructions.

At that moment, what went through Candide's mind, and his way of logically analyzing the situation, were as follows:

"If this holy man calls for help, he'll surely have me burned at the stake; he might even do the same thing to Cunégonde; he had me brutally whipped; he's my rival; I've already killed one man, and I can't afford to hesitate."

His thinking was clear and quick: without giving the Inquisitor time to recover from his shock, he ran him through and tossed him onto the floor, alongside the Jew.

"So now we've got another one," said Cunégonde. "There'll be no more forgiveness; we're excommunicated, our last hour has come. How can it be that you, born so sweet and gentle, have in two minutes managed to kill a Jew and a priest?"

"My dear girl," answered Candide, "a man who's in love, who's jealous, and who's been whipped by the Inquisition, is out of his mind."

Then the old woman took charge, saying:

"There are three Spanish horses in the stables, with their saddles and bridles. Let our brave Candide make them ready. Madame has gold and diamonds. Quickly, let's mount and—though I've only got one buttock—let's ride to Cadiz. The weather is perfectly lovely, and how pleasant it is to travel in the quiet freshness of night."

Candide immediately saddled the three horses. Cunégonde, the old woman, and he rode thirty miles without stopping. While they were dashing away, the police came to the house. The Inquisitor was buried at a lovely church, and Issacar was thrown into the garbage dump.

Candide, Cunégonde, and the old woman were by that time in the little town of Avacena, deep in the Sierra Morena mountains, and seated in an inn, they were speaking as follows:

Chapter Ten

In what difficulty Candide, Cunégonde, and the old woman reached Cadiz, and how they boarded a ship

"Who stole my gold and my diamonds?" said Cunégonde, weeping. "What will we live on? What will we do? Where can we find inquisitors and Jews who'll give me more?"

"Alas!" said the old woman. "I strongly suspect the thief was a respectable Franciscan priest who lodged yesterday in the inn with us, in Badajoz. God save me from a rash, reckless judgment! But he came into our room twice, and he left a long time before we did."

"Ah!" said Candide. "How often Pangloss explained to me that earthly possessions belong to all men in common, with everyone having equal rights. According to these principles, the Franciscan really should have left us enough to make our voyage. He left you nothing at all, my lovely Cunégonde?"

"Not a penny," she said.

"What should we do?" said Candide.

"Sell one of our horses," said the old woman. "I'll ride behind Miss Cunégonde (although I have only one buttock), and we'll get to Cadiz."

There was a Benedictine prior in the same establishment, and he bought the horse for a very good price. Candide, Cunégonde, and the old woman rode through Lucena, through Chillas, through Lebrixa, and finally arrived at Cadiz. There was a ship being readied, and troops were being collected, in order to bring the Jesuit priests of Paraguay to their senses: they were accused of having incited one of the native tribes, near the town of San Sacramento, to rebel against the Kings of Spain and Portugal. Having served with the Bulgars, Candide performed the Bulgarian drill in front of this little army's general, and with such polish, such dispatch, such skill, such fire, such agility, that he was made a captain and given an infantry company to command. He embarked with Cunégonde, the old woman, two valets, and the two Spanish horses, once the property of Portugal's Grand Inquisitor.

As they sailed across the ocean, they spent a great deal of time discussing poor Pangloss's philosophy.

"We're going to a different universe," said Candide. "Surely that's where everything is for the best. And I confess we do have to groan a little, at what goes on in ours, in matters both physical and moral."

"I love you with all my heart," said Cunégonde. "But my soul is still terrified of what I've seen, and what I've experienced."

"It's going to be better," said Candide. "The ocean in this new world is already better than the one in our Europe. It's calmer, the wind is steadier. Oh, definitely: the new world is the best of all possible universes."

"May God so will it!" said Cunégonde. "But I've been so horribly miserable, in my world, that my heart is almost closed against hope."

"You complain," the old woman told them. "Alas! You've never experienced misfortunes like mine."

Cunégonde felt like laughing: the old woman struck her as amusing, trying to make herself appear worse off than her mistress.

"Oh, my dear," she told the old woman. "Unless you've been raped by *two* Bulgars, been stabbed—*twice*—in the belly, watched *two* of your mansions torn apart, seen *two* mothers and *two* fathers have their throats cut right in front of you, and witnessed *two* of your dearly beloveds being flogged in an auto-da-fé—well, I don't see how you can get the better of me. And when you add that I was born a baroness, and my lineage is seventy-two-percent pure, and that I've actually been a cook . . . ."

"Madame," said the old woman, "you have no knowledge of my birth—and were I to show you my bottom, you would not speak as you just did, you would be obliged to suspend judgment."

These words sparked an extraordinary curiosity in Cunégonde and Candide. What the old woman told them was as follows:

Chapter Eleven
The old woman's story

"I haven't always had bloodshot, red-rimmed eyes; my nose hasn't always drooped onto my chin; and I haven't always been a servant. I am the daughter of Pope Urban the Tenth and the Princess of Palestrina. I was brought up, until the age of fourteen, in a palace that none of your German baronial mansions could have served as a stable, and one of my gowns would have been worth more than all the splendors of Westphalia. I grew in beauty, in elegance, in accomplishment, in the midst of pleasure, respect, and hope. I had already inspired love, my breasts had ripened—and what breasts! White, firm, shaped like those of the Medici Venus. And what eyes! what eyelashes! what gorgeous black eyebrows! What brilliance flashed from my pupils, gleaming brighter than stars—as the local poets used to assure me. The women who dressed me, and undressed me, fell into ecstasies, observing me from the front and from the rear, and there wasn't a man who did not yearn to be in their place.

"I was engaged to a royal prince of Massa-Carrara. And what a prince! He was my match in beauty, fashioned of sweetness and charm, with a brilliant mind, and burning with love. I loved him as one loves for the first time, worshipfully, ecstatically. Our wedding ceremony had been readied. It was to be a display, an unheard-of magnificence. There were to be banquets, tournaments, never-ending performances of comic operas, and all Italy wrote sonnets about me, not one of which was even worth remembering.

"I was at the very threshold of happiness, when an old marquise who'd been my prince's mistress was invited to take chocolate with him. He died less than two hours later, in ghastly convulsions. But that's just a detail. My mother, in great despair, but nothing compared to mine, felt the need to spend some time away from so funereal a setting. She owned an exceedingly beautiful estate, near Gaeta, just north of Naples. We set sail on a local ship, gilded like Saint Peter's altar in Rome. And then a Moroccan pirate came sailing at us, and the pirates swarmed on board. Our guards defended us like papal soldiers: they knelt down, threw away their weapons, and begged the pirates for absolution before they were killed.

"The pirates promptly stripped them as naked as monkeys, and my mother, too, and all our maids of honor, and me. It is truly remarkable how diligent these fellows are, when it comes to stripping people. But what startled me even more was how they stuck their fingers in a place where we women usually allow only the nozzle of a syringe. This was a ritual that struck me as exceedingly odd: that's of course how one views everything, when traveling abroad for the first time. I soon learned they wanted to see whether we'd hidden diamonds in there. This is an established and immemorial custom among all the civilized nations that sail the seas. I was informed that the religious Knights of Malta never failed to observe it, whenever they captured Turkish men and Turkish women: it is indeed an international law never infringed upon.

"I won't bother telling you how insufferable it is for a young princess, enslaved in Morocco along with, of all people, her mother. You can imagine perfectly well what we had to endure on that pirate vessel. My mother was still quite pretty; our maids of honor, even our chambermaids, were lovelier than the women one might find anywhere in all Africa. As for myself, I was ravishing, I was beauty and grace incarnate, and I was a virgin. I was not a virgin for long: that flower, reserved for the handsome Prince of Massa-Carrara, was stolen from me by the pirate captain, a disgusting black man who, nevertheless, thought he was showing me high honor. Clearly, the Princess of Palestrina and I had to be enormously strong to endure what we experienced on the voyage to Morocco. But let it pass: these are such common matters that they're not even worth mentioning.

"Morocco was swimming in blood when we arrived. Each of the fifty sons of Emperor Muley-Ismail had his own following, which in effect produced fifty civil wars—black against black, black against brown, brown against brown, mulatto against mulatto. The carnage was continual, across the entire empire.

"We were barely off the boat when the blacks from another faction came to relieve my pirate of his booty. Next to diamonds and gold, we were the most precious commodities he had. I witnessed fighting you'll never see in Europe: the blood of our northern nations simply isn't hot enough. Lust for women doesn't burn in them as it does in Africans. Europeans seem to have milk in their veins, but it's vitriol and fire flowing in the veins of those who live in and around the Atlas Mountains. They fought over us with the fury of their native tigers and lions and snakes. A Moor grabbed my mother's right arm, my captain's chief lieutenant held her left one. A Moorish soldier took her by the leg, and one of our pirates clutched the other one. In a flash, virtually all our maids were pounced on from four different sides. My captain hid me behind his back, wielding a scimitar and killing anyone who tried to get around him. Finally, I saw all our Italian women as well as my mother ripped up, chopped, sliced, massacred by the monsters who were competing for them. Those who'd captured us—soldiers, sailors, blacks, browns, whites, mulattos, and in the end my captain—were killed, and I was left dying on a pile of corpses. Scenes exactly parallel took place, of course, for at least a thousand miles in all directions, though they were always interrupted for the five daily prayers commanded by Mohammed.

"With considerable difficulty, I got down from the crowded heap of bloody corpses and dragged myself under a tall orange tree, next to a little stream. I fainted from fright, weakness, horror, despair, and hunger. Soon, my overwhelmed senses brought me to a sleep that contained more weakness than it did repose. I was in exactly that state of feeble unknowingness, hovering between death and life, when I felt myself squeezed by something that twisted and turned on my body. I opened my eyes, I saw a good-looking white man, and heard him sighing, in Italian, between clenched teeth: *O che sciagura d'essere senza c* . . . 'O what a disaster, not to have testicles . . .' "

Chapter Twelve

More about the old woman's misfortunes

"Astonished, and delighted, to hear my native language, and no less surprised by the words the man spoke, I replied that there were worse misfortunes than the one he complained about. I gave him a succinct account of the horrors I had suffered, and dropped back into unconsciousness.

"He carried me into a nearby house, put me to bed, gave me food, took care of me, consoled me, flattered me, said he had never seen anything as beautiful as me, and said that never had he so bitterly regretted what no one could ever give him back.

" 'I was born in Naples,' he told me, 'where they castrate two or three thousand children a year. Some of them die; others develop voices more beautiful than women's; some rule kingdoms. My operation was highly successful: I became a chapel musician to the Princess of Palestrina.'

" 'My mother's musician!' I cried.

" 'Your mother!' he exclaimed, weeping. 'What! You were that young princess I carried around until she was six years old, who already showed promise of becoming as beautiful as you are now?'

" 'That was me. My mother is four hundred paces from here, cut to pieces and lying under a pile of corpses . . . .'

"I told him everything I'd experienced; he in turn told me his adventures, telling me a Christian power had sent him to the King of Morocco, in order to negotiate a treaty giving Morocco powder and cannons and ships, so trade with other Christian states could be wiped out.

" 'My mission is complete,' this worthy eunuch told me. 'I'll be sailing from Ceuta, and I'll bring you back to Italy. *Ma che sciagura d'essere senza c . . . !* But what a disaster not to have testicles!'

"I thanked him with my tenderest tears. And instead of taking me to Italy, he brought me to Algeria and sold me to the Governor. I had just been sold when the plague, which had struck Africa, Asia, and Europe, began to rage through Algeria. You've seen earthquakes, Miss. But have you ever had the plague?"

"Never," answered the Baroness.

"If you had," resumed the old woman, "you'd admit it was far worse than an earthquake. It's extremely common in Africa, and I caught it. Just imagine being a pope's daughter, fifteen years old, who in three months' time had experienced poverty, slavery, who had been raped almost daily, who had seen her mother chopped into four pieces, had suffered hunger and war, and was dying of plague in

Algeria. However, I did not die. But my eunuch, and the Governor, and almost the entire harem, perished.

"Once the initial ravages of this ghastly disease had passed, they sold the Governor's slaves. A merchant bought me and took me to Tunis. He sold me to another merchant who took me to Tripoli. From Tripoli I was re-sold to Alexandria, from Alexandria re-sold to Smyrna, from Smyrna to Constantinople. In the end I belonged to a general of the Turkish Sultan's Guard, who soon after was ordered to proceed to the defense of Azov, which the Russians had besieged.

"The General was a very dashing man, and took his entire personal harem with him, installing us in a little fort on the Sea of Azov, guarded by two black eunuchs and twenty soldiers. A great many Russians were killed, but the Russians gave as good as they got. Azov was burned and bloodied, and no one was exempted on account of their sex or their age. All that remained standing was our little fort, which the Russians proposed to starve into submission. Our twenty Turkish soldiers had sworn never to surrender. They were reduced to such extremities that, in order to preserve their oath, they were obliged to eat the two eunuchs. Some days later, they decided to eat the women.

"There was an Islamic priest with us, a very pious and compassionate man, and he preached them a handsome sermon, trying to persuade them not to simply kill us. 'Just cut off,' he said, 'one buttock from each of the women, which will provide you with excellent food. If it turns out, some days later, that you need more, there will be just as much more still available. Heaven will be pleased by so charitable a deed, and you will be saved.'

"He was a very eloquent man; he convinced them. The soldiers performed the horrible operation on us. The priest applied the same medicine used on children who have just been circumcised. We were all of us near death.

"The Turkish soldiers had no sooner finished the meal we'd provided them when the Russians attacked, using flat-bottomed boats. Not one Turkish soldier survived. The Russians paid not the slightest attention to the condition we were in. There were French doctors accompanying them, and one of them, very skillful, took care of us. He cured us, and I will remember as long as I live that, once our wounds had healed, he propositioned me. Besides, he told us, we shouldn't feel too bad: in many other sieges, he declared, exactly the same thing had happened, this being the laws of warfare.

"When my companions were able to walk, we were forced to go to Moscow. I ended up as the property of a petty nobleman, who made me his gardener and gave me twenty lashes a day. But when, two years later, this gentleman was broken on the wheel, along with thirty other nobles, for some petty problem at the Tsar's court, I took advantage of his misfortune and ran off. I went right across Russia; for a long time I worked in an inn in Riga, then at Rostock, at Wismar, at Leipzig, at Kassel, at Utrecht, at Leyden, at the Hague, at Rotterdam. I've grown old in misery and dishonor, with only half a backside, always reminding myself that I was the daughter of a pope. A hundred times I wanted to kill myself, but I loved life too much.

This ridiculous weakness may be one of our most dismal tendencies: is there anything stupider, actually *wanting* to go on carrying a burden you constantly long to throw to the ground? than being horrified by your existence, and yet holding onto it? and in the end to caress the serpent as it devours us, until it's eaten all the way to the heart?

"In the countries Fate swept me through, and in the inns where I labored, I've seen a tremendous number of people who hate their lives, but I've only seen a dozen who voluntarily put an end to their misery: three Negroes, four Englishmen, four Swiss, and a German professor named Robeck who'd written a book about suicide. I finally became servant to a Jew, Don Issacar, and he brought me, my dear young lady, to you. I've now been linked to your destiny, and indeed I've been more concerned with your affairs than my own. I'd certainly never have spoken of my misfortunes if you hadn't annoyed me a little bit and if it hadn't been customary, traveling on boats, to chase away boredom by telling your life story.

"To conclude: I've had experience, I know the world. Amuse yourself, ask every passenger to tell you his story, and if you find one, just one, who hasn't often cursed his life, who hasn't often told himself he's the unluckiest of men, throw me headfirst into the sea."

Chapter Thirteen

How Candide was forced to leave lovely Cunégonde and the old woman

Lovely Cunégonde, having heard the old woman's story, accorded her all the courtesies owed to a person of her rank and worth. And she accepted the old woman's challenge, asking all the passengers, one after the other, to tell her their stories. She and Candide then agreed that the old woman had been right.

"What a shame," Candide said, "that wise Pangloss was hanged, against the rules of the auto-da-fé. He would have told us marvelous things about the physical and moral evil that covers both earth and sea, and I would have felt myself strong enough to dare, most respectfully, to present him with a few objections."

As each person was telling his story, the ship sailed on. They landed in Buenos Aires. Cunégonde, along with Captain Candide and the old woman, paid a call to the Governor, Don Fernando d'Ibaraa, y Figueora, y Mascarenes, y Lampourdos, y Souza. This gentleman had the pride proper to a man who bore so many names. He spoke down to others with the very noblest disdain, raising his nose high in the air, mercilessly elevating his voice, taking on a tone so imposing, putting on a manner so lofty, that anyone greeting him was tempted to hit him. He was wildly fond of women. Cunégonde seemed to him the most beautiful he had ever seen. The first question he asked was whether she was the captain's wife. The fact that he asked this question worried Candide. He did not dare say she was his wife, since in fact she wasn't. He did not dare say she was his sister, because that would have been no more truthful. And even though white lies had once been very much in fashion, among the ancients, and might conceivably prove useful to contemporaries, too, his heart was too pure to commit treason against the truth.

"Miss Cunégonde," he said, "if you'll do me the honor of becoming my wife, we will beg Your Excellency to perform the ceremony."

Don Fernando d'Ibaraa, y Figueora, y Mascarenes, y Lampourdos, y Souza tweaked his moustache, smiled wryly and ordered Captain Candide to go review his troops. Candide obeyed; the Governor remained with Miss Cunégonde. He declared his love, saying he would marry her the next day, in church or out, however so dazzling a lady might desire. Cunégonde asked for a quarter of an hour to collect herself, to consult with the old woman, and to make up her mind.

The old woman told her:

"Miss, you are seventy-two percent noble and don't have a cent. Whether or not you marry the greatest lord in South America—who has an extraordinarily handsome moustache—is entirely up to you. Is it appropriate to pride yourself on perfect faithfulness? You've been raped by Bulgars; a Jew and an inquisitor have had your favors. Misfortunes create prerogatives. I confess that, if I had the opportunity, I would not hesitate to marry the Governor and make Captain Candide's fortune."

As the old woman was speaking, with the good sense acquired by age and experience, a small ship sailed into the harbor, carrying a sheriff and several policemen—and here is what had happened:

The old woman had guessed, very correctly, that it was a Jesuit with long sleeves who stole Cunégonde's gold and diamonds, in the town of Badajoz, as they were fleeing with Candide. This monk had tried to sell several diamonds to a jeweler who had recognized the Grand Inquisitor's jewels. Before he was hanged, the Jesuit had confessed his theft and identified those from whom he had stolen and the route they were traveling. Cunégonde and Candide's flight was already known to the authorities. They were followed to Cadiz and a ship sent at once to pursue them. This was the vessel that had just arrived in Buenos Aires. A rumor had already spread that a sheriff was on the ship, chasing after the Grand Inquisitor's murderers.

The canny old woman instantly realized what had to be done.

"You can't run away," she told Cunégonde, "and you don't have to be afraid. You weren't the murderer, and besides, the Governor loves you and won't let you be mistreated. Stay here."

The old woman went running to Candide.

"Run," she said, "or in another hour you'll be burned at the stake."

There was not a moment to waste. But how could he leave Cunégonde? And where could he seek refuge?

Chapter Fourteen

How Candide and Cacambo were greeted by the Jesuits of Paraguay

Candide had brought with him, from Cadiz, a valet of a type often found on the coasts of Spain and in the colonies. He was one-quarter Spanish, born to a half-breed in Tucuman. He'd been a choirboy, a sacristan, a sailor, a monk, a broker, a soldier, a servant. His name was Cacambo, and he was wonderfully fond of Candide, because his master was a truly good man.

He quickly saddled both their horses.

"Let's go, my master: let's take the old woman's advice. Let's get out of here and ride as hard as we can, and never look behind us."

Candide wept.

"O my dear Cunégonde! Must I abandon you just when the Governor is about to perform our marriage? Led here from so far away, O Cunégonde, what will become of you?"

"She'll do whatever she can," said Cacambo. "Women never have to worry, God takes care of them. Let's go."

"Where are you taking me? Where are you going? What will we do without Cunégonde?" said Candide.

"In the name of Saint James of Compostela!" said Cacambo. "You were going to fight against the Jesuits: let's go fight for them. I know how to get there, I'll bring you to their kingdom. They'll be thrilled to have a captain who knows the Bulgar drills; you'll make a ton of money. When you can't make a splash in one world, you find your-self a different one. It's great fun, seeing and doing new things."

"So you've already been in Paraguay?" asked Candide.

"Good Lord, yes!" said Cacambo. "I served in their Assumption school, and I know how the Jesuits work every bit as well as I know the streets in Cadiz. It's really a fantastic thing, that govern-ment. The kingdom is already more than four hundred miles across; they've divided it into thirty provinces. The priests are everything, the people don't count. The place is a masterpiece of reason and justice. Me, I've never seen anything as close to God as the Jesuits. Over here, they're fighting against the King of Spain and the King of Portugal; over in Europe, they hear kings' confessions. They kill Spaniards, over here, and back in Madrid they send them to heaven. I love it! Let's go. You'll be the happiest man alive. How tickled the Jesuits are going to be, getting a captain who knows the Bulgar drills!"

The moment they arrived at the first outpost, Cacambo told the frontier guards that a captain wanted to speak to their commander. They went to advise the chief sentry. A Paraguayan officer ran on foot, bringing the news to the commander. First, Candide and Cacambo were disarmed; their Spanish horses were taken away. The strangers were led in, between two columns of soldiers; the com-mander stood at the end of the line, a three-cornered cap on his head, his long coat tucked up, a sword at his side, a cross-barred, shafted pike in his hand. He gave a sign; immediately, twenty-four soldiers surrounded the newcomers. A sergeant told them they had to wait, the commander could not speak to them, and the Jesuit in charge of the province prohibited any Spaniard from opening his mouth, except in the presence of the priest himself, nor to remain among them for longer than three hours.

"And where is the Jesuit?" said Cacambo.

"He's reviewing the troops, having just said Mass," replied the sergeant. "And it will be three hours before you're allowed to kiss his spurs."

"However," said Cacambo, "the captain—who is dying of hunger, as I am also—is emphatically not Spanish: he is German. Can't we have breakfast while we're waiting for the holy man?"

The sergeant immediately went to report this to the commander.

"Blessèd God!" said the commander. "Since he's German, I can speak to him. Have him brought to my covered arbor."

Candide was immediately taken to this leafy office, decorated with a very pretty colonnade of green and gold marble and by latticework, inside which were parrots, all sorts of hummingbirds, guinea fowl, and a host of rare and unusual birds. A first-rate breakfast was waiting, in golden bowls, and while the Paraguayans ate corn out of wooden bowls out in the fields and in the blazing sun, the commander walked into the arbor.

He was a very handsome young man, with a rather plump face, quite white, high-colored, his eyebrows arched, eyes gleaming, ears red, lips vermilion, his demeanor proud, but displaying neither the pride of a Spaniard nor that of a Jesuit. Candide and Cacambo were given back their weapons, and also their Spanish horses, to which Cacambo fed oats, outside the arbor, alertly watchful, fearful of some surprise.

Candide first kissed the hem of the commander's cassock, and then they sat at table together.

"So you're German?" said the commander, speaking in that language.

"Yes, Father," said Candide.

They looked at one another, as they spoke, with immense surprise and an emotion they could neither of them control.

"And what part of Germany are you from?" said the Jesuit.

"The filthy province of Westphalia," said Candide. "I was born in the mansion of Thunder-den-tronckh."

"O heaven!" exclaimed the commander. "Is this possible?"

"What a miracle!" cried Candide.

"Is it really you?" said the commander.

"This is not possible," said Candide.

They both fell down, they got up, they embraced, they shed streams of tears.

"What! It's you, my Reverend Father? you, lovely Cunégonde's brother! you, who were killed by the Bulgars! you, the Baron's son! you, a Jesuit in Paraguay! This world, it must be conceded, is a very strange place. O Pangloss! Pangloss! How happy you'd be, if you hadn't been hanged!"

The Negro slaves were sent away, and also the Paraguayans who filled the crystal goblets. The Jesuit thanked God and Saint Ignatius a thousand times; he hugged Candide tightly; their faces were awash with tears.

"You'd be even more astonished," said Candide, "if I were to tell you that Miss Cunégonde, your sister, who you thought had been disemboweled, was in excellent health."

"Where?"

"In your part of the world, with the Governor in Buenos Aires. And I crossed the ocean to make war on you."

Every word they exchanged, in this long conversation, piled wonder on wonder. Their souls flew out on their tongues, listening closely in their ears, glittering in their eyes. Being Germans, they sat at table a long time, while waiting for the Jesuit in charge of the province, and this is what the commander told his dear Candide:

Chapter Fifteen
How Candide killed his dear Cunégonde's brother

"I will remember as long as I live that horrible day when I saw my father and mother killed and my sister violated. When the Bulgars left, that adorable girl was nowhere to be found, and they put us in a cart, my mother, my father, and me, plus two servants and three little boys with their throats slit, to bury us all in a Jesuit chapel a few miles from my ancestral mansion. A Jesuit sprinkled us with holy water, which was horribly salty; several drops got in my eyes;

the priest noticed my eye twitching. He put his hand on my heart and felt it beating; I was saved, and three weeks later, I was as good as new.

"You know, my dear Candide, that I was an exceedingly pretty child, and I became even prettier, so the Reverend Father Croust, the Jesuit Superior, developed a most tender fondness for me. He put me in a novice's cassock, and not too long afterward I was sent to Rome. The Father General of the order needed new recruits from the young German Jesuits. The rulers of Paraguay take as few Spanish Jesuits as they can; they prefer foreigners, thinking they can more readily control them. The Reverend Father General found me fit to go and labor in this vineyard. We left, one Pole, one Tyrolean, and me. I was honored, on my arrival, by being made an assistant deacon and a lieutenant; I am now a colonel and a priest. We will give the King of Spain's soldiers a brisk welcome: I can assure you they'll be excommunicated and beaten. Providence sent you here, to assist us.

"But is it really true that my dear sister, Cunégonde, is not far away from here, with the Governor at Buenos Aires?"

Candide swore that nothing could be truer. Their tears began to fall, once more.

The Baron couldn't stop embracing Candide, calling him his savior, his brother.

"Ah, perhaps," he said, "we may be together, my dear Candide, entering that city as conquerors, and bringing back my sister, Cunégonde."

"That's all I want," said Candide, "because I've been counting on marrying her, and I still expect to."

"You, insolent rascal!" replied the Baron. "You'd have the impudence to marry my sister, who's of seventy-two-percent noble blood! That's damned cheeky—you dare speak to me in such ridiculous terms!"

Struck almost dumb by these words, Candide answered:

"My dear Father, noble birth doesn't apply. I drew your sister out of the arms of a Jew and an inquisitor. She owes me a great deal, and she wants to marry me. Doctor Pangloss always told me that men were born equal—and yes, I certainly will marry her."

"That's what you think, you scoundrel!" said the Jesuit Baron Thunder-den-tronckh, simultaneously cracking Candide across the face with the flat side of his sword. Candide promptly pulled out his own weapon and buried it to the hilt in the Jesuit Baron's belly. But then, as he pulled his sword out again, still smoking, he began to weep.

"Alas! My God," he said. "I've killed my former master, my friend, my brother-in-law. I'm the nicest man in the world, and this is the third man I've killed—and two of three were priests."

Cacambo, who'd been standing sentinel outside the arbor, came running in.

"All that's left is to sell our lives as dearly as we can," his master told him. "They'll surely be coming in here. We must die with our weapons in our hands."

Cacambo, who had seen a great deal, did not lose his head. He took the Jesuit robe off the Baron and put it on Candide, gave him the dead man's square cap, and had him mount the Baron's horse. It was all done in a twinkling of an eyelash.

"Let's gallop, my master. They'll think you're a Jesuit going to give orders, and we'll be across the frontier before they can chase after us.

He was already flying even as he spoke these words, shouting in Spanish:

"Make way, make way, for the Reverend Father colonel!"

Chapter Sixteen

What happened to the two travelers with two girls, two monkeys, and the savages known as Oreillons

Candide and his valet were past the frontiers, and still no one in the camp knew the German Jesuit was dead. Cacambo, ever alert, had taken care to fill his traveling bag with bread, chocolate, ham, fruit, and several containers of wine. They pushed through the forest on their Spanish horses, crossing through an unknown land and finding no road. Finally, they came to a lovely meadow, crisscrossed with streams. Our two travelers fed their horses. Cacambo suggested to his master that they too feed themselves, and promptly set the example.

"How," said Candide, "can you expect me to sit here, eating ham, when I've just killed the Baron's son and know I'm condemned not to see my lovely Cunégonde for the rest of my life? What's the point to prolonging my miserable days, when I'm obliged to drag myself through them, far from her, in unending remorse and despair? And what will *The Jesuit Journal* say?"

He'd begun to eat, as he was saying these words. The sun went down. The two wanderers heard little screams, apparently uttered by women. They couldn't tell if these were cries of pain or of pleasure, but they rose hurriedly, troubled by the uncertainty and concern that everything in an unknown country produces. The sounds were coming from two stark-naked girls, running nimbly at the edge of the meadow, followed by two monkeys who were nipping at their backsides. Candide was struck with pity. The Bulgars had taught him how to shoot, and he could have knocked a nut out of a bush without hitting a leaf. He picked up his double-barreled Spanish gun, fired, and killed the two monkeys.

"God be praised, my dear Cacambo! I've freed those two poor creatures from immense danger. If I've sinned, killing a Jesuit and an inquisitor, I've surely made up for it by saving those girls' lives. They may even be young ladies of high rank, and this affair might do us a lot of good, here in this country."

He meant to say more, but his tongue turned stiff when he saw the two girls tenderly embracing the monkeys, raining tears on their bodies and filling the air with the most heartrending sobs.

"I never expected such soulful generosity," he said to Cacambo, at last.

His valet answered:

"That was a masterful piece of work, my master. You've killed these young ladies' lovers."

"Their lovers! Is that possible? You're making fun of me, Cacambo. There's no way I can believe that."

"My dear master," Cacambo replied. "You're always astonished, no matter what happens. Why do you think it so strange that countries exist where monkeys make love to women? They're one-quarter human, just as I'm one-quarter Spanish."

"Alas!" Candide answered. "I remember hearing Maître Pangloss say that sometimes such accidents happen and that such cross-breeding produces Pans, fauns, satyrs, and that great men, in ancient times, saw these things. But I took it for fairy tales."

"You ought to be persuaded, now," said Cacambo, "that it's the truth, and you see how people act, when they haven't had a real education. All I'm worried about is that these ladies don't do something wicked to us."

These eminently sensible reflections led Candide to leave the prairie and take them deep into the forest. He and Cacambo ate their supper, and having cursed the Portuguese Inquisitor, the Governor at Buenos Aires, and the Baron, they both fell asleep on the moss. When they awoke, they realized they could not move a muscle, the reason being that, during the night, the natives of that country, the Oreillons, to whom the young ladies had denounced them, had tied them up with tree-bark ropes. They were surrounded by fifty or so naked Oreillons, carrying spears, clubs, and flint axes. Some were heating up a huge cauldron, others were preparing wooden spits, and all of them were screaming:

"A Jesuit, a Jesuit! We'll be revenged, and we'll have a feast! Eat the Jesuit, eat the Jesuit!"

"I told you the truth, my dear master," exclaimed Cacambo sadly. "I told you those two girls would do us a dirty trick."

Noting the cauldron and the spits, Candide cried:

"We're surely going to be roasted, or perhaps boiled. Ah! What would Maître Pangloss say if he saw how pure nature works? Everything is for the best—fine. But I confess it seems really cruel to have lost Miss Cunégonde and to be turned on a spit by Oreillons."

Cacambo never lost his head.

"Don't worry about it," he told our miserable Candide. "I understand a bit of these people's language. I'm going to have a chat with them."

"Don't forget to tell them," said Candide, "that it's frightfully inhuman to cook people, and not very Christian, either."

"Gentlemen," said Cacambo. "Today, you're expecting to eat a Jesuit. That's fine: nothing is fairer than to deal with your enemies like that. In fact, natural law teaches us to kill our fellow man, and that's how the whole world has always acted. If we Europeans don't exercise this right, it's because we have other things to feast on. And it's surely better to eat our enemies than to leave the fruits of our victory for the crows and ravens. However, gentlemen, you should not eat your friends. You *think* you're going to roast a Jesuit, but you'll be roasting your true champion, your enemy's enemy. Me,

I was born in your country. The gentleman you see, who's with me, is my master, and far from being a Jesuit, he has just killed a Jesuit and stripped him naked. This, then, is the victim of your hatred. To confirm what I'm telling you, simply take his uniform, carry it to the first frontier post of the Jesuit kingdom, and find out if my master really did kill a Jesuit. It won't take long: you can always eat us if you find I've lied. But if I've told you the truth, you understand too well the principles of public justice, and of manners, and of law in general, not to show us mercy."

The Oreillons thought this was entirely reasonable. They authorized two leading personages to go, with all due speed, and find out the facts. Like true men of spirit, the two performed their mission and quickly returned, bearing good news. The Oreillons freed their prisoners, treated them with every possible courtesy, offered them their women, gave them refreshments, and then conducted them to the borders of their land, crying joyfully:

"He's not a Jesuit, he's not a Jesuit!"

Candide could not restrain his amazement at being thus delivered.

"What a race!" he said. "What men! What manners! If I hadn't had the luck of running Miss Cunégonde's brother right through, with a great thrust of my sword, I'd have been eaten, there'd have been no stopping them. But after all, pure nature is indeed good, since these people, rather than eating me, have treated me with immense respect, once they realized I was not a Jesuit."

Chapter Seventeen

Arrival of Candide and his valet in the land of Eldorado, and
what they saw there

When they'd reached the Oreillian border:

"You can see," Cacambo said to Candide, "that this hemisphere is
no better than the other one. Believe me, let's go back to Europe as
fast as we can."

"How can we go back?" said Candide. "And where could we go?
If I go to my own country, the Bulgars and the Abars are cutting
every throat they see. If I go to Portugal, I'd be burned alive. If we
stay where we are, we risk at any moment being put to the spit. But
how can I make up my mind to leave the part of the world occupied
by Miss Cunégonde?"

"Let's head for Cayenne," said Cacambo. "We'll find Frenchmen,
there, who travel all over the world. They'll be able to help. Maybe
God will take pity on us."

Going to Cayenne was not easy. They knew pretty well what
coast they had to proceed toward, but the mountains, rivers, steep
cliffs, the thieves and savages, were singularly horrific obstacles.
Their horses died of weariness; they ate their entire supply of food;
they endured for an entire month on nothing but wild fruit, and
finally arrived at a small river bordered by coconut palms, which
preserved both their lives and their hopes.

Cacambo, whose advice was always just as good as the old woman's, said to Candide:

"We can't go any farther, we've walked more than far enough. I see an empty canoe on the riverbank. Let's fill it with coconuts, throw ourselves in that little boat, and float with the current. Rivers always lead to some inhabited place. If we don't find pleasant things, we'll at least find new ones."

"Let's go," said Candide, "and may Providence guide us."

They floated for some miles, sometimes between flower-covered banks, sometimes between barren ones; some were flat and level, some were craggy and steep. The river kept growing larger, and finally disappeared under dreadful, soaring rocks that rose almost to the sky. The two travelers had the courage to let the waves take them under this high, rocky arch. Drawing narrower as it swept down, the river carried them with ghastly speed, and to the accompaniment of a horrible, crashing din. After twenty-four hours, they came back up to the light of day, but their canoe was smashed to pieces on reefs. For an entire mile, they were forced to crawl from one rock to another, and finally discovered an apparently endless horizon, bordered by unclimbable mountains. The country was cultivated as much for delight as for food, and everywhere that which was useful was also good to see. Roadways were covered—really, ornamented—by vehicles of a gleaming material, brilliantly shaped, and bearing men and women of exceptional beauty; these carriages were pulled by great red horses, which ran faster than the finest steeds of Spain or Morocco.

"Now here," said Candide, "is a country considerably superior to Westphalia."

They started toward the first village they could see. There were children, covered with badly ripped gold brocade, playing quoits near the entranceway. Our two visitors from another world amused themselves, watching. The children's large rings—yellow, red, and green—gleamed most remarkably. The travelers were moved to pick up a few of these strange toys, which turned out to be gold, emeralds, and rubies, the smallest of which would have been major ornaments of the Mogul Emperor's throne.

"Surely," said Cacambo, "we must be watching the King's sons, playing quoits with rings like these."

The village schoolmaster appeared, just then, to bring the children back to school.

"Ah," said Candide. "This must be the royal tutor."

The little rascals immediately broke off their game, leaving their rings and other toys where they lay. Candide collected them, ran to the tutor, and respectfully handed them over, indicating by gestures that Their Royal Highnesses had forgotten their gold and jewels. The schoolmaster, laughing, threw the stuff on the ground, stopped for a moment to look, with much surprise, at Candide's face, and then followed his pupils into their school.

The travelers gathered up a good deal of gold, and rubies, and emeralds.

"Where are we?" exclaimed Candide. "These royal children must be extremely well bred, since they're being taught to scorn gold and jewels."

Cacambo was just as startled as his master.

At last, they came to a large dwelling, built like a European palace. A crowd was hurrying to the door, and there were many more people inside. They could hear very charming music, and they smelled delicious food being cooked. Cacambo went over to the door and heard them speaking Peruvian, his native tongue—for as everyone knows, Cacambo was born in Tucuman, in a village where no other language was understood.

"I'll be your interpreter," he told Candide. "Let's go in. This is an inn."

Immediately, two young men and two girls, wearing golden cloth, their hair tied back with ribbons, invited them to take a table. They were served four soups, each garnished with a pair of parrots; a boiled condor that weighed two hundred pounds; two roasted monkeys, beautifully seasoned; three hundred large hummingbirds on a platter, and six hundred small ones on another, plus several superb ragouts, and some excellent pastry. And they ate from crystal plates and bowls. The young men and the girls came back, repeatedly, to fill their glasses with various drinks prepared from sugarcane.

The other diners were for the most part merchants and teamsters, all extraordinarily courteous. They asked Cacambo a few questions, with the utmost discretion, and answered each of his queries to his complete satisfaction.

When they had finished eating, Cacambo and Candide both thought it proper to pay their bill by depositing on the table two of the large chunks of gold they had gathered. The host and hostess doubled over with laughter, and for a long time had to hold their sides. Finally, they got themselves under control:

"Gentlemen," said the host, "we see perfectly well that you are strangers. We're not accustomed to the sight. Forgive us if we laughed, when you tried to pay us with pebbles collected off the roadways. I've no doubt you have none of our money, but you don't need any, to dine here. All inns created for the convenience of businesspeople are funded by the government. You haven't eaten particularly well, here, because ours is only a poor little village, but anywhere else you'll be received as you deserve to be."

Cacambo explained this whole speech to his master, and Candide listened in the same bewildered wonderment his friend had displayed, translating it.

"What is this place," they asked each other, "totally unknown to the rest of the world, and so utterly unlike what we're accustomed to? It must be the country where everything is indeed for the best, since there absolutely has to be a place of that sort."

"And what would Maître Pangloss say," added Candide, "since I often saw how badly everything goes, in Westphalia."

Chapter Eighteen

What they saw in Eldorado

Cacambo told their host how very curious he was, and the host replied:

"I'm very ignorant, and very comfortable the way I am. But there's an old man, here in our village, who's retired from the King's court, and he's the most learned man in the whole country, and the most talkative."

He immediately took Cacambo to the old man. Candide had become no more than a secondary personage, merely an accompaniment to his valet. They came to an extremely plain house, the door being ordinary gold, as were the interior walls, yet all worked with such fine taste that even truly expensive homes would not have put the place to shame. The entrance hall, it must be conceded, was merely inlaid with rubies and emeralds, but the justness of their ordering redeemed such extreme simplicity.

Seated on a sofa stuffed with hummingbird feathers, the old man received the two travelers, and offered them drinks in diamond containers, after which he satisfied their curiosity in these words:

"I'm a hundred and seventy-two years old. I learned from my late father, Master of the King's Horses, about the astonishing rebellions in Peru, of which he was a witness. Our kingdom, here, is the ancient realm of the Incas, from which they went forth, most rashly, to subjugate a fair part of the world. They were ultimately destroyed by the Spaniards.

"The princes of the royal family who chose to remain in their original land were wiser. It was their decree, with the consent of all the inhabitants, that no citizen was ever to leave our small kingdom, and that's what has preserved our innocence and our happiness. The Spanish had some uncertain knowledge of this land, which they called El Dorado, and there was an Englishman, one Sir Walter Raleigh, who ventured quite close to it, perhaps a hundred years ago. However, since we are surrounded by unclimbable rocks and cliffs, we have always been—to this very day—sheltered from the rapacity of Europe, which has an incredible passion for the pebbles and mud of our land, to possess which they would kill us all, to the last living soul."

It was a long conversation, dealing with governmental form, with manners, women, public spectacles, and with the arts. At last Candide, who had never lost his taste for metaphysics, had Cacambo ask, on his behalf, if the country had a religion.

The old man's face reddened.

"Indeed," he said, "how could you doubt it? Do you take us for ingrates?"

Cacambo asked, very respectfully, what their religion was.

The old man's face remained flushed.

"Is it possible to have two religions?" he said. "We have the same religion, I believe, that the entire world has: from dawn to dusk, we adore God."

"But do you adore just one God?" asked Cacambo, still interpreting Candide's doubts.

"Obviously," said the old man, "since there are neither two, nor three, nor four. I must confess that the people of your world ask very strange questions."

But Candide did not give up in his interrogation of the good old man. He wanted to know how one prayed to God, here in Eldorado.

"We don't pray to him at all," said the good and honorable sage. "We have nothing to request of him. He has given us everything we need. We thank him ceaselessly."

Candide was curious to see their priests, and asked where they were.

The good old man smiled.

"My friends," he said, "we are all priests. Every morning, the King, and every head of a family, sing solemn hymns in praise of the great blessings with which God has showered us. And they are accompanied by five or six thousand musicians."

"My Lord! You have no monks to teach, to argue, to govern, and to plot, and to burn alive those who don't share their views."

"We'd have to be out of our minds," said the old man. "Everyone here is of exactly the same opinion, and no one would understand you when you talk about your monks."

Candide had listened to every word in sheer ecstasy. He said to himself:

"This is not a bit like Westphalia or the Baron's mansion. Had our friend Pangloss seen Eldorado, he'd have stopped saying that Thunder-den-tronckh was the finest mansion in the world. One certainly must travel, in order to understand!"

At the end of this long conversation, the old man called for a coach pulled by six sheep and lent the two travelers a dozen of his servants to conduct them to the royal court.

"Excuse me," he told them, "if my years deprive me of the honor of accompanying you. The King will receive you so well that you will not be dissatisfied, and if there are any of our country's habits and customs which displease you, you will forgive us."

Candide and Cacambo climbed into the coach; the six sheep fairly flew; and in less than four hours they arrived at the King's palace, located at one end of the capitol city. The entrance was two hundred and twenty feet high, and a hundred feet wide; it is impossible to say in mere words of what materials it was constructed. But it was easy to see how immensely superior it was, compared to the pebbles and the sand we call *gold* and *jewels*.

Twenty beautiful girls, of the King's Guards, welcomed Candide and Cacambo as they descended from the coach, then conducted them to the baths, dressed them in garments made of hummingbird feathers, woven into cloth, after which the chief Royal Officers, male and female, conducted them to His Majesty's suite, accompanied by two lines of a thousand marching musicians each, as was the usual custom. As they drew near the throne room, Cacambo asked one of the Chief Officers how one was supposed to behave, greeting His

Majesty. Did protocol require that they kneel, or throw themselves down, face first? Would they place their hands on their head, or hold them behind their back? Were they supposed to lick the dust on the floor? In a word, what was the customary ritual?

"The custom," said the Chief Officer, "is to embrace the King and kiss him on both cheeks."

Candide and Cacambo threw their arms around the King, who welcomed them with perfect courtesy and politely asked them to dinner.

While waiting, they were given a tour of the city. Its public buildings towered almost to the clouds, its marketplaces were decorated with a thousand columns. Some of the fountains spouted jets of clear water, some threw up rose-tinted water, some exhaled drinks made from sugarcane—and all were in continuous operation in the great central plazas, which were paved with aromatic rock, giving off a fragrance very like cloves and cinnamon. Candide asked to be shown a law court and the country's parliament, but he was informed that neither existed, nor did law suits. He then inquired if they had prisons, and they replied that they did not. But what most surprised and most deeply pleased him was the Palace of Science, in which he saw a gallery two thousand feet long, filled with instruments employed in mathematics and physics.

Having traveled over perhaps a thousandth part of the city, that afternoon, they were brought back to the royal palace. Candide was seated with the King, his valet, Cacambo, and a number of ladies.

The meal was superb, and no one had ever enjoyed himself more than the King, whose clever witticisms were explained for Candide by Cacambo. No matter how translated, they still survived as bon mots. Of all the things that astonished Candide, this was certainly not the least.

They enjoyed this hospitality for a month, and Candide never stopped saying to Cacambo:

"It's worth saying yet again, my friend, that the mansion in which I was born wouldn't be worth much where we now are, but Miss Cunégonde isn't here, and surely you have a mistress somewhere in Europe. If we remain here, we'll be no different from anyone else. But if we go back to our own world, with just a dozen sheep loaded with Eldorado's pebbles, we'll be richer than all the kings of Europe put together, and we won't have to be afraid of any inquisitors, and we'll have no trouble getting back Miss Cunégonde."

These remarks pleased Cacambo. It is only natural, wanting to show off what you've come home with, and making a great fuss over all you've seen in your travels, so these two happy men decided not to be happy any longer and to request the King's permission to leave.

"That would be a serious mistake," the King told them. "I quite understand that my little country is nothing very much, but when a man is doing reasonably well, wherever he may be, it's a great deal better to stay there. On the other hand, I certainly have no right to detain strangers: that is a tyranny we neither practice nor have ever considered practicing. All men are free: you may leave whenever you like. But leaving will not be easy. It would be impossible to go back on the swift stream by means of which, through some miracle, you reached here. The mountains surrounding my kingdom are ten thousand feet high and as sheer as walls. Each of them is twenty-five miles wide, and you can descend only via the steepest of precipices.

"However, if you're truly determined to leave, I'll instruct the Managers of Machinery to design an apparatus for you, capable of bringing you comfortably across. But, having brought you to the other side of the mountains, no one will be able to accompany you any farther: my subjects have taken an oath never to leave their surroundings, and they're far too sensible to break that oath.

"Now, if there is anything else you require, please just ask me."

"We request of Your Majesty," said Cacambo, "some sheep loaded with food, with pebbles, and with the mud and muck of this country."

The King laughed.

"I cannot understand," he said, "what you Europeans see in our yellow mud. But take as much as you like, and much good may it do you."

Then and there, he ordered his engineers to fashion a machine to lift these two extraordinary men out of the kingdom. Three thousand good scientists worked at it. After two weeks, they had it ready, and at a cost of no more than twenty million pounds sterling, in their own currency. Candide and Cacambo were placed in the machine, along with two very large red sheep, saddled and bridled, meant for them to ride on once they had crossed the mountains; twenty packsaddle sheep, loaded with food; thirty carrying gifts of the country's most unusual and interesting wares; and fifty bearing gold, jewels, and diamonds. The King embraced the two wanderers most tenderly.

Their departure was a splendid spectacle, as was the ingenious fashion in which they were hoisted, they and their sheep, as high as the highest mountains. The engineers said farewell, once the travelers had been safely deposited on the other side, and Candide wanted nothing more than to offer his sheep to Miss Cunégonde.

"Whatever we might need to pay the Governor at Buenos Aires," he said, "if Miss Cunégonde has been taken prisoner, we have more than enough to pay it. Let's proceed to Cayenne and get ourselves a ship, and then we can find out which kingdom we'll be able to buy."

Chapter Nineteen

How they got to Surinam, and how Candide came to know Martin

The two travelers' first day was pleasant enough. They were cheered by the thought of possessing treasure richer than anything Asia, Europe, and Africa together could have acquired. Candide, absolutely carried away, wrote Cunégonde's name on trees.

On the second day, two of their sheep sank in the marshes and disappeared, along with everything they were carrying; several days later, two more sheep died of weariness; seven or eight, still later, perished in a desert, of starvation; not long after, more of them fell off cliffs. Finally, a hundred days into their journey, all they had left were two sheep.

Candide said to Cacambo:

"My friend, you can see how the riches of this world crumble away. Nothing is really solid except virtue and the delight of seeing Miss Cunégonde again."

"I admit it," said Cacambo. "But we still have two sheep, with more treasure than the King of Spain will ever have, and I see a city in the distance, which I suspect is Surinam, a Dutch colony. We are at the end of our suffering and the beginning of our happiness."

As they drew closer to the city, they encountered a Negro, stretched out on the ground, wearing no more than half his clothing—that being a pair of blue shorts. The poor fellow had lost his left leg and his right hand.

"O my God!" said Candide, speaking to him in Dutch. "What has brought you, my friend, to the horrible condition I see you are in?"

"I'm waiting for my master," the Negro replied, "the celebrated merchant, Monsieur Vanderdendur."

"And is it Monsieur Vanderdendur," said Candide, "who has treated you like this?"

"Yes, sir," said the Negro. "That's the way it's done. Clothing is given to us twice a year: that means a pair of blue shorts. When we're working in the sugar mills and the grinding wheel catches a finger, they cut off a hand. When we try to escape, they cut off a leg. Both things have happened to me. This is what it costs, supplying you Europeans with sugar.

"But when my mother sold me for ten silver coins, on the Guinea coast, she said to me:

" 'My dear child, worship our tribal gods, adore them forever, they will make your life happy, for you have the honor of being a slave to our lords the white men, and in the process you have made your father and your mother's fortune.'

"Alas! I don't know if I made their fortune, but they haven't made mine. Dogs, monkeys, and parrots are a thousand times less miserable than we are. The Dutch witchdoctors who converted me say to us, every Sunday, that we're all children of Adam, both blacks and whites. But if these preachers are telling the truth, we're all cousins once removed. Just tell me, sir, how parents could treat their children any worse."

"O Pangloss!" exclaimed Candide. "You never imagined such an abomination. If this truly happened, I have no choice but to abandon your optimism."

"What's optimism?" asked Cacambo.

"Lord help me," said Candide, "it's the madness of insisting that everything is good when it's bad."

And he wept, looking at the Negro, and was still weeping when he reached Surinam.

The very first thing they looked for was a ship that might be going to Buenos Aires. The man from whom they sought this information turned out to be himself a Spanish captain, who offered to make them a good, honest bargain. He proposed that they discuss it at an inn. Candide and his faithful Cacambo went there to wait for him, along with their sheep. Candide, whose heart was in his mouth, told the Spaniard everything, and admitted that he meant to run off with Miss Cunégonde.

"I'll be very careful not to carry you to Buenos Aires," said the captain. "I'd be hanged, and so would you. Pretty Cunégonde is the Governor's favorite mistress."

This hit Candide like a thunderbolt; he wept for a long time. Finally, he led Cacambo aside.

"Now, my dear friend," he said, "here's what you have to do. We've each got five or six millions of diamonds in our pockets. And you're smarter than I am. So you go to Buenos Aires and get Miss Cunégonde. If the Governor makes any difficulties, give him a million. If he won't let you have her, give him two million. You weren't the one who killed the Inquisitor, they aren't going to ask any questions about you. I'll get myself another boat, and I'll go wait in Venice. That's a free country, and you don't have to worry about Bulgars, or Abars, or Jews, or inquisitors."

Cacambo approved of this sensible solution. He was miserable at the thought of going away from his master, who had become his close friend, but the pleasure of being useful to Candide drove away his sadness. They embraced each other, both of them weeping. Candide reminded him not to forget the good old woman. Cacambo left that very day: he was a very good man, this Cacambo.

Candide stayed in Surinam a bit longer, waiting for another captain who'd take him to Italy, along with the two remaining sheep. He hired servants and bought everything he'd need on a long voyage. At last, Monsieur Vanderdendur, captain and owner of a large ship, came to him.

"How much do you want," Candide asked, "to take me straight to Venice—me, my servants, my baggage, and those two sheep over there?"

The captain proposed ten thousand Spanish pesos. Candide did not hesitate.

"Oh ho!" said careful Vanderdendur to himself. "This foreigner's ready to pay ten thousand pesos, just like that! He must be rich as the devil."

So, after just a moment, he came back, indicating he could not set sail for less than twenty thousand.

"All right! That's what you'll get," said Candide.

"Oh really!" the merchant murmured to himself. "This fellow pays twenty thousand just as easy as ten thousand."

So, once more, he turned and came right back, saying he simply couldn't take Candide to Venice for less than thirty thousand.

"All right," said Candide. "You can have thirty thousand."

"La, la!" the Dutch merchant said to himself. "Thirty thousand pesos are like nothing to this man. Obviously, those two sheep are loaded with incredible treasures. All right, we won't ask for any more. Let's get those thirty thousand pesos—and after that, well, we'll see."

Candide sold two small diamonds, the smaller of which was worth more than everything the captain had asked. And he paid in advance. The two sheep were brought on board. Candide followed after, on a little boat, intending to board the ship just before it got to open water. The captain seemed in no hurry. Then suddenly, on a favorable wind, he set his sails and was off to sea. Shocked, stunned, Candide soon lost sight of the ship.

"Alas!" he exclaimed. "This is a trick worthy of the old world."

He returned to the harbor, overwhelmingly sorrowful, having lost treasures worth the fortunes of twenty kings.

He went at once to the Dutch judge and, because he was rather upset, knocked at the judge's door a little loudly. He was admitted, explained what his business was, and spoke in a voice just a touch more elevated than was entirely proper. The judge began by fining him ten thousand pesos for all the noise he'd made. Then he listened patiently, promised to look into the affair as soon as the merchant returned, and made Candide pay an additional ten thousand pesos to defray costs.

The whole affair brought Candide to the point of desperation. Truthfully, he'd experienced sorrows a thousand times worse, but the judge's total indifference, as well as that of the thieving captain, brought his bile to the boil, driving him into a profound melancholy. Human wickedness, in all its ugliness, became glaringly clear to him; his mind fed exclusively on dismal thoughts.

At last, there being a French ship ready to sail for Bordeaux, he booked himself a cabin—having no more sheep loaded with diamonds—at a fair price. Then he let it be known that he'd pay the passage, food, and give two thousand pesos in addition to a respectable man who would accompany him, provided that the applicant proved himself the man who, of anyone in the entire country, was sickest of his life there, and the most miserable.

There were crowds of candidates, more than a whole flotilla could have carried. Trying to single out the most obvious choices, Candide picked twenty who seemed to him sufficiently sociable, each and all of whom claimed to deserve the honor. He brought them to an inn, gave them dinner, requiring only that each man swore to give a faithful account of his life history. He promised to choose whoever struck him as having the most to complain of, and was the most completely discontented, for good and sound reasons. He also promised to pay a gratuity to those who were not selected.

The session lasted until four o'clock in the morning. Listening to all their stories, Candide reminded himself of what the old woman told him, as they were sailing to Buenos Aires, and the bet she'd made, that there wouldn't be a single person on board the vessel who hadn't experienced immense misfortune. And he also thought of Pangloss, as he heard each life history.

"Our Pangloss," he told himself, "would be seriously embarrassed, trying to prove his philosophy. Plainly, if there is a place where everything is for the best, it has to be Eldorado and nowhere else on earth."

His choice fell, in the end, on a poor scholar who'd spent ten years working in the bookshops of Amsterdam. It was Candide's opinion that there was no more disgusting trade in the world, so this man had to be the most discontented of all.

The scholar (who was also a good man) had been robbed by his wife, beaten by his son, and deserted by his daughter, who'd run off with a Portuguese. He had just lost the petty job he'd been living on, and the Surinam priests persecuted him as a heretic. He realized that the others were at least as miserable, but Candide hoped the scholar he'd chosen would save him from boredom on the long voyage. Every one of the others was convinced Candide had done them a vast injustice, but they felt better after he gave them a hundred pesos apiece.

Chapter Twenty

What happened at sea to Candide and Martin

And so the old scholar, whose name was Martin, set sail for Bordeaux with Candide. They'd both seen and suffered a great deal, and even if the ship had left Surinam, headed first to Japan by way of the Cape of Good Hope, they'd have had quite enough experience of immorality and misery to last them the whole voyage.

Yet Candide had one large advantage over Martin, which was that he never gave up hope of seeing Miss Cunégonde again; Martin had absolutely nothing to hope for. What's more, Candide had gold and diamonds, and even though he'd lost a hundred fat red sheep, loaded with the greatest treasures in the world, and even though his heart remained heavy at the Dutch captain's wickedness, still, whenever he considered what was still in his pockets, and talked about Cunégonde—especially at the end of a meal—he pondered Pangloss's philosophic system:

"But you, sir," he said to the scholar, "how does all that strike you? What is your position on immorality and misery?"

"Sir," replied Martin, "our priests accused me of being a rationalist, one who denied Christ's divine nature. But the truth is that I believe everything is equally divided between good and evil."

"You're pulling my leg," said Candide. "You a Manichean? There aren't any left."

"There's me," said Martin. "What can I do about it? I believe what I believe."

"You must be possessed by Satan," said Candide.

"He's so active in this world," said Martin, "that he could very well be inside me, since he's everywhere else. But I must say that, looking at our globe—or, rather, our globule—it seems to me that God has surely abandoned it, except of course for Eldorado, to *some* evil being. I've virtually never seen a city that doesn't yearn for the ruin of the city next to it, or a family that doesn't want to exterminate another family. Everywhere you look, the prostrated powerless are silently cursing the powerful, who treat them like flocks, selling their wool and their meat. A million uniformed assassins go running from one end of Europe to the other, earning their bread by murdering and robbing—with military discipline—because there isn't any more honorable profession. And in places where people seem to be living in peace, and the arts are flourishing, they're more devoured by jealousy, and worry, and uncertainty than the scourges that fall on a city under siege. Secret sorrows are far crueler than public miseries. In short, it's because I've seen so much evil, and experienced so much, that I'm a Manichean."

"But everywhere you look," said Candide, "there's goodness, too."

"Conceivably," said Martin. "But I have no knowledge of it."

In the middle of this discussion, they heard the boom of a cannon. The sounds grew louder and louder. Everyone raised a spyglass. They saw two ships, in combat at a distance of roughly three miles; the wind blew them so close to the French vessel that, completely divorced from the fighting, they nevertheless had the pleasure of a fine view. Finally, one of the vessels fired a broadside so well aimed at the water line that the other ship began to sink. Candide and Martin could distinctly see a hundred men on the deck of the boat going under, men who were lifting their hands to heaven and screaming frightfully. And then, in an instant, they were all of them drowned.

"Well!" said Martin. "That's how human beings treat each other."

"Yes," said Candide, "there's certainly something diabolic about this kind of thing."

As they were talking, they saw who knows what gleaming red object swimming toward their own ship. The longboat was lowered, so they could find out what this was. It was one of Candide's sheep.

He felt greater happiness, getting back this sheep, than the sorrow he'd experienced, losing a hundred of them, loaded with huge Eldorado diamonds.

The French captain soon realized that the captain of the victorious vessel was Spanish, and the captain of the sunken one had been a Dutch pirate—the very same man who had robbed Candide. The immense wealth stolen by this scoundrel had sunk to the bottom, along with him. Only one single sheep had survived.

"You see," said Candide to Martin, "how sometimes crime is indeed punished. This rascal of a Dutch captain met the fate he deserved."

"Yes," said Martin. "But was it necessary that the passengers on board his ship die with him? God punished this scoundrel; the devil drowned the others."

So the French vessel, like the Spanish one, went on its way, and Candide continued his conversations with Martin. They argued for fifteen days in a row, and at the end of fifteen days were exactly where they'd been when they started. Then they really talked, exchanging ideas and consoling each other. Candide stroked his sheep.

"Since I've gotten you back," he said, "maybe I'll get Cunégonde, too."

Chapter Twenty-one

Candide and Martin approach the French coast and argue

At last, they could see the French coast.

"Have you ever been to France, sir?" Candide asked.

"Yes," said Martin. "I passed through several provinces. In some, half the inhabitants were insane; in others, people were incredibly crafty; in a few, everyone was distinctly pleasant and just as distinctly stupid; elsewhere, everyone was terribly witty; and in every single province the primary occupation was love, followed by lying, and after that by the speaking of utter idiocies."

"But sir, did you get to see Paris?"

"O yes, I saw Paris. They've got all kinds there. It's certified chaos, a mob where everyone's hungry for pleasure and where virtually no one finds it—or so it seemed to me. I did not stay long. When I first arrived, pickpockets at the Saint-Germain market stole everything I had. I myself was taken for a thief, and I spent a week in prison. Then I worked as a printer's proofreader, to earn enough so I could cross into Holland, on foot. I got to know the scribbling scum, the scheming scum, and the raving lunatic scum. They say the city boasts some people of profound good manners. I expect there are."

"Myself," said Candide, "I haven't the slightest interest in seeing France. You can quite understand how, after spending a month in Eldorado, there's no longer any desire to see anything on earth, except Miss Cunégonde. I'll be waiting for her at Venice. We'll be crossing France on our way to Italy. Why don't you come with me?"

"Gladly," said Martin. "It's said that Venice is only livable for aristocratic Venetians, but that foreigners are very well received, when they have enough money. I haven't any, you do, so I'll follow you everywhere."

"By the way," said Candide. "Do you think the earth was originally covered by water, as claimed in this fat book, which I've borrowed from our captain?"

"I don't believe a word of it," said Martin, "any more than I believe all the daydreams they're always trying to sell us."

"But why then was this world put here?" asked Candide.

"To drive us wild," answered Martin.

"Weren't you shocked," Candide went on, "by those two Oreillon girls who loved a pair of monkeys, as I've already told you?"

"Not at all," said Martin. "I fail to see what's strange about such a passion. I've seen so many extraordinary things, by now, that nothing seems extraordinary."

"Do you believe," asked Candide, "that men have always massacred one another, as we saw earlier today? That they've always been liars, swindlers, traitors, ingrates, thieves, weak-minded, cowards, full of envy, gluttons, drunks, misers, pushing and shoving to get ahead, bloodthirsty, slanderers, rakes, fanatics, hypocrites, and fools?"

"Do you believe," said Martin, "that hawks have always eaten all the pigeons they can find?"

"Yes, certainly," said Candide.

"So there you are!" said Martin. "If hawks have always stayed the same, why do you expect men to change?"

"Oh," said Candide. "There's a big difference, because free will . . . ."

They were still arguing when the ship reached Bordeaux.

Chapter Twenty-two

What happened to Candide and Martin in France

Candide lingered in Bordeaux just long enough to sell some of his Eldorado pebbles and to get himself a good light carriage, with two seats, for he could not have managed, now, without his philosopher, Martin. But he deeply regretted having to leave his sheep, which he gave to the Bordeaux Academy of Science. The Academy's prize, that year, was given for an explanation of why the Eldorado sheep was red and was won by a northern scholar, who demonstrated by A plus B, minus C, divided by Z, that the sheep had to be red, and would ultimately die of sheep pox.

Still, all the travelers Candide met at inns along the way told him they were going to Paris. In the end, such a universal fuss made him want to see the capital city; it would not be a serious detour from the road to Venice.

He entered Paris through the suburb of Saint Marceau and felt as if he was in the ugliest town in Westphalia.

He'd barely settled himself in his lodgings when he was attacked by a minor illness, brought on by fatigue. Since he wore an enormous diamond on his finger, and since it had been noticed that his carriage contained an exceedingly heavy jewelry box, he was immediately attended by two physicians, whose presence he had not requested, several intimate friends who would not leave him, and two intensely devoted ladies who heated up his soup. Martin observed:

"I remember being sick myself, on my first visit to Paris. I was terribly poor, so I had no friends, no devoted ladies, no doctors, and I got better."

However, on account of the medicines and the bleedings, Candide's illness turned serious. A local priest, who had no parish, came to sweetly request a promissory note, payable to bearer in another world. Candide said he'd give him nothing. The devoted ladies assured him this was not the ways things were usually done; Candide replied that he was not interested in how things were usually done. Martin said he'd be glad to throw the priest out the window. The priest swore Candide would never be buried in hallowed ground. Martin swore he'd bury the priest if he did not leave them alone. The quarrel grew heated; Martin caught the priest by the shoulder and shoved him out; this created an immense scandal and led to a police report.

Candide recovered, and as he convalesced enjoyed a good deal of company. They gambled, and for high stakes. Candide was astounded that he never got any high cards, and Martin was not a bit astounded.

Among those who lavished local hospitality on him was a little priest from Périgord, hyperactive, always both watchful and ready, always helpful, brassy, flattering, completely flexible—one of those who keep an eye out for strangers, tell them racy stories about Paris, and supply entertainment at any cost.

He began by taking Candide and Martin to the theater. A new tragedy had just opened. Candide found himself sitting near some Parisian wits. This did not keep him from weeping at perfectly acted scenes. At an intermission, one of the quibblers told him:

"You were ridiculous, weeping like that. That actress is absolutely awful, and the actor playing opposite her is even worse; the play is still worse; the author doesn't know a word of Arabic, though the scene is supposed to be Arabia—and what's worst of all, he quite rejects Descartes' view of the mind and accepts Locke's. Tomorrow I'll bring you twenty pamphlets that totally expose him."

"Sir," Candide asked his Périgord priest, "how many plays have been written in France?"

"Five or six thousand," was the reply.

"That's a lot," said Candide. "How many of them are any good?"

"Fifteen or sixteen."

"That's a lot," said Martin.

Candide was struck by an actress, who several times played the role of Queen Elizabeth in a distinctly dull tragedy.

"I like that actress," he told Martin. "She reminds me of Miss Cunégonde. I would much like to tell her so, in person."

The Périgord priest offered to conduct him to her house and introduce him.

Candide, having been raised in Germany, wondered about propriety, and also about how English queens were treated in France.

"You need to draw some distinctions," said the priest. "Outside of Paris, you take them to an inn. Here in Paris, you deal with them respectfully, while they're still beautiful, and when they're dead you throw them on the garbage heap."

"Throw queens in the garbage!" said Candide.

"Yes, of course," said Martin. "Our priest is quite right. I was in Paris when Miss Monime passed, as they put it, from this life to the next. She was refused what those people term 'the rights of burial' — which in fact only means rotting with all the local beggars in a shabby cemetery. So she was buried, completely alone, at the corner of rue de Bourgogne. For someone with so noble a mind, it must have been deeply painful."

"How terribly rude," said Candide.

"What can you expect?" said Martin. "That's what these people are. Conjure up every conceivable contradiction, every possible inconsistency — and there it all is, right in the government, the courts, the churches, in all the sights and displays of this amusing nation."

"Is it true that people in Paris are always laughing?" asked Candide.

"Yes," said the Périgord priest. "But in anger, because they complain about everything, yet always in gales of laughter. And they laugh even when they're committing utterly detestable acts."

"Who is that fat pig," said Candide, "who said such nasty things about the play, and those wonderful actors, when he saw me so moved that I wept?"

"He's a walking disease," the priest answered, "who earns his bread by saying horrible things about plays and books. He hates whoever is successful, the way eunuchs hate happier men. He's one of those literary snakes, feeding on muck and poison. He's a hack."

"What does that mean, a 'hack'?" said Candide.

"Someone who produces polluted pages, like that fraud Fréron."[1]

Which is how Candide, Martin, and the Périgord priest chatted, descending the stairs and watching the other theatergoers leaving.

"No matter how anxious I am to see Miss Cunégonde again," said Candide, "I'd like to dine with Miss Clairon. I thought she was wonderful."

The priest could not get near Miss Clairon, since she saw only the best people.

"She has an engagement tonight," he said. "But let me bring you to a very fine lady, in whose house you'll learn as much of Paris as if you'd spent four years in the city."

Candide, who was by nature curious, allowed himself to be shown to the lady's house, at the far end of the faubourg Saint-Honoré. The people there were deeply engrossed in playing faro, twelve wretched men, each holding a small hand of cards—ridiculous registers of

---

1. A distinguished critic with whom Voltaire waged incessant war.

their woes—as they bet against the game's banker. The silence was deathly; the bettors' faces were pale; the banker's face was worried; and the lady of the house, seated near the banker (who was merciless), followed every bet with eyes like a lynx, noting every ploy, every maneuver, honest or dishonest—and sternly, though politely, made them undo every flagrant violation, always remaining cool and unconcerned about losing her clients. She called herself Marquise de Parolignac. Her fifteen-year-old daughter, one of the bettors, signaled the others' miserable little tricks, informing her mother, with a wink, of their struggles against a cruel fate.

The Périgord priest, with Candide and Martin, entered the room. No one rose, no one greeted them, no one so much as noticed them, so deeply were they sunk in their card game.

"Baroness Thunder-den-tronckh was a good deal more polite," said Candide.

Still, the priest bent to the Marquise's ear, and the lady half rose, honoring Candide with a gracious smile, and Martin with a profoundly aristocratic glance. She offered Candide a chair and a chance to play; he lost fifty thousand francs in two deals, after which they all joined in a delightful supper, everyone stunned that Candide was not upset at his loss. The servants murmured among themselves, in the language of servants:

"He's got to be an English nobleman."

Their supper was like most Parisian suppers, opening with silence, which was followed, first, by such a barrage of words that nothing could be understood, and then by witticisms, most of them insipid, founded in ignorant gossip, horrible logic—a dash of politics and a lot of slander. They even talked about new books.

"Has anyone," asked the Périgord priest, "read the new novel by someone named Gauchat,[2] a doctor of theology?"

"Yes," said one of the guests. "But I couldn't get through it. We certainly have a horde of insolent writers, but added all together they can't come close to this Gauchat, doctor of theology. I'm so sick of such heaps of unreadable pages, burying us under their weight, that I've decided simply to play faro."

"And what do you think of Archdeacon Trublet's[3] volume of essays?" asked the priest.

"Ah!" said Madame de Parolignac. "Such deadly boredom! How quaintly he tells you what everyone already knows! How ponderously he pores over what's not worth so much as a passing glance! How lifelessly he sucks up others' quick wit! How he ruins everything he steals! How he disgusts me! But he won't get the chance again: having read a few pages of the archdeacon's pages is quite sufficient . . . ."

A scholar of good taste, seated among them, concurred with the Marquise.

And then they discussed tragedies. The lady of the house wondered why they were afflicted with performances of unreadable trag-

2. Gabriel Gauchat, another of Voltaire's many enemies.
3. And yet another bitter enemy.

edies. The scholar explained, very neatly, that a play might well have something interesting about it, but no literary value. He demonstrated, without wasting words, that a playwright had to do more than throw in some of the complications found in all novels, and perpetually attractive to theater audiences. Playwrights had to be novel without being bizarre, frequently sublime but never unnatural; they had to understand the human heart and let it speak for itself; they had to be great poets but never let any of their characters sound like poets; they had to perfectly understand language and use it purely, with continuous harmony, never disjointing it with forced rhyme.

"A playwright," he added, "who ignores any of these rules may have a success or two, but he'll never be considered a significant writer. There are very few good tragedies: many are just nicely rhymed poems, spoken in dialogue; others are political tracts that put us to sleep, or expanded arguments that soon grow tedious; we have ranting daydreams, written barbarically, in totally confused sequence, with long-winded apostrophes to God—because they have no idea how to speak to men—decked out with fake wisdom and reams of bombastic clichés."

Candide listened most attentively to these remarks, and developed a high opinion of the speaker. And since the Marquise had carefully seated him right next to her, he bent over and, whispering, took the liberty of asking who he was, this man who talked so brilliantly.

"A scholar," replied the lady, "who never gambles; the priest from

Périgord sometimes brings him for dinner. He has a masterful under-standing of tragedy, and of literature: a tragedy of his was produced, and hissed off the stage, and a published book was seen outside the bookshop only in a copy he'd inscribed to me."

"What a great man!" said Candide. "He's a new Pangloss."

Then, addressing the mighty scholar, he said:

"Sir, I'm sure you believe that everything is for the best, both in the moral and the physical world, and that nothing could possibly be different?"

"I, sir," the scholar answered, "think nothing of the sort. I think everything goes wrong, in this world of ours; that no one under-stands either his place or his duties, and except for dinner—which is cheerful and appears to bring people together—we spend our time in ridiculous quarrels. We have Puritans fighting with Jesuits, parlia-mentarians fighting with bishops, writers fighting with other writ-ers, and courtesans with other courtesans; we have bankers fighting the people, women fighting against their husbands, relatives against other relatives. What we have, in short, is endless warfare."

Candide replied:

"I've seen worse things. But a very wise man, who suffered the misfortune of being hanged, taught me that all these things are truly fine: they're shadows of a lovely painting."

"Your hanged man," said Martin, "was poking fun at the world. Your shadows are really ghastly stains."

"It's men who make the stains," said Candide, "and they have no choice."

"Then it's not their fault," said Martin.

Most of the gamblers, who heard not a word of all this, were busy drinking; Martin argued with the scholar; and Candide told the lady of the house some of his adventures.

Afterwards, the lady led Candide to her private room and seated him on a sofa.

"Now!" she said. "You've always been wildly in love with Miss Cunégonde, of Thunder-den-tronckh?"

"Yes, madame," said Candide.

The Marquise, smiling tenderly at him, replied:

"You've answered me like a young man from Westphalia. A Frenchman would have said: 'It's true, I've loved Miss Cunégonde, but now that I've seen you, madame, I think I've stopped loving her.'"

"Ah, madame!" exclaimed Candide, "I'll tell you whatever you want to be told."

"Your passion for her," said the Marquise, "began when you picked up her handkerchief. I'd like you to pick up my garter."

"With great pleasure," said Candide, picking it up.

"But I want you to give it back to me," said the lady, and Candide gave it back to her.

"You see," the lady told him, "you're a foreigner. I've often made my Parisian lovers languish for a week or two, but I'll give myself to you the very first night, because a young man from Westphalia deserves the honors of the country."

The pretty lady, having observed the enormous diamonds Candide wore, one on each hand, admired them with such sincerity that they moved from Candide's fingers to hers.

Going home afterward, with his Périgord priest, Candide felt a certain remorse at having been unfaithful to Miss Cunégonde. The priest shared his sorrow: he'd gathered in only a small share of Candide's fifty-thousand-franc gambling loss, and of the value of the two diamonds, half of which was given, half extorted. He meant his acquaintance with Candide to bring him all the profit he could get. He entered into a long conversation about Miss Cunégonde, Candide informing him that he'd certainly beg the beautiful woman's pardon, on account of his infidelity, as soon as he saw her in Venice.

The priest became even more courteous and attentive, displaying deep, concerned interest in everything Candide told him, in everything Candide had done, in everything Candide meant to do.

"So you'll have a rendezvous in Venice?" he asked.

"Yes, Father," said Candide. "It's absolutely essential that I go find her."

Then, caught up in the pleasure of speaking about his beloved, Candide narrated, as was his habit, some of his adventures with this illustrious Westphalian lady.

"I suspect," said the priest, "that Miss Cunégonde has a first-class mind and writes charming letters?"

"I've never had any from her," said Candide. "Remember: having been driven away from Thunder-den-tronckh, on account of my love for her, it became impossible to write; not long after I heard she was dead, I found her again; and then I lost her; and I've now written to her, from two thousand, five hundred miles away, and sent my letter by the fastest ship available, and here I am, in Paris, waiting for her answer."

The priest listened attentively, apparently rather lost in reflection. He soon said goodnight to the two strangers, having first embraced them with great tenderness.

The next day, Candide received the following letter:

"Sir, My dearest love, I've now spent a week in this city, sick in bed. I'm told you too are here. I'd fly into your arms, if I were able to move. They tell me you came by way of Bordeaux, where I left faithful Cacambo and the old woman, who are soon to follow me here. The Governor in Buenos Aires has taken everything, leaving me only your heart. Come to me, your presence will bring me back to life, or at least let me die happily."

This charming missive, this totally unexpected letter, swept Candide into inexpressible joy, just as his dear Cunégonde's illness filled him with sadness. Torn between these two emotions, he took his gold and his diamonds and, together with Martin, had himself conducted to the hotel where Miss Cunégonde was staying. Trembling with emotion, he entered her room, his heart beating hard, his voice breaking. He started to open the bed curtains and let in a bit of light.

"Be very careful," said the nurse. "Light will kill her."

And she quickly closed the curtains.

"My dear Cunégonde," said Candide, weeping, "how are you? If you're not allowed to see me, at least speak to me."

Chapter Twenty-two

"She's unable to speak," said the nurse.

Then, from behind the curtains, the desperately sick lady stretched out a plump hand, which Candide watered with his tears. After a long, long time, he filled the plump hand full of diamonds and, leaving a purse filled with gold on the arm chair, had just left the room when a police officer appeared, followed by the Périgord priest and a squad of uniformed men.

"So," said the officer, "these are the two suspicious foreigners?"

He immediately ordered his brave men to seize Candide and Martin and haul them off to prison.

"Travelers aren't treated like this," said Candide, "in Eldorado."

"I believe more profoundly than ever in the power of evil," said Martin.

"My dear sir," said Candide, "where are you taking us?"

"To a dungeon cell," said the officer.

Having collected his wits, Martin realized that the lady pretending to be Cunégonde was a thieving fraud; their good friend, the Périgord priest, was a thieving rascal who had taken swift advantage of Candide's innocence; and the officer was another thieving rascal who could easily be gotten rid of.

Rather than risk the workings of justice, and acting on Martin's advice, Candide—anxious as always to find the real Cunégonde—presented the officer with three small diamonds, each worth three thousand gold coins.

"Ah, sir!" the man with the ivory nightstick exclaimed. "Even if you'd committed every crime imaginable, you are clearly the most respectable man in the world! Three diamonds! Each one worth three thousand gold coins! Sir! Rather than take you to jail, I'd kill myself for you. We normally arrest foreigners the minute we see them, but I'll take care of that. I have a brother at Dieppe, in Normandy, and I'll bring you there, and if you've got another diamond for him, he'll take just the same care of you that I would myself."

"But why do you arrest foreigners on sight?" said Candide. The Périgord priest then took the floor, saying:

"It's because a beggar from Arras heard a lot of nonsense, and it made him kill his father—not the kind of murder committed in May 1610 but, rather, the sort perpetrated in December 1594 and, of course, several others also committed in different years and in different months by other beggars who paid attention to a lot of nonsense."

Then the officer explained what the priest was talking about.

"O, what monsters!" Candide cried. "What! Such horrors committed by a nation of people who sing and dance! I have to get away, as fast as I can, from a country where monkeys infuriate tigers! I've seen bears in my birthplace; the only place I've ever seen men is Eldorado. Ah, in the name of God, Mr. Officer, take me to Venice, where I'm going to wait for Miss Cunégonde."

"The only place I can take you to," said the officer, "is Lower Normandy."

So he had the chains taken off them, apologized for having put them on in the first place, sent his men away, and brought Candide and Martin to Dieppe, leaving them there and in his brother's hands.

There was a small Dutch ship in the harbor. Motivated by another three diamonds, the Norman brother had become the most helpful of men; he put Candide and his people on this little boat, which was heading for Portsmouth, in England. It was not the most direct route to Venice, but Candide had been saved from hell and certainly meant to resume his journey to Italy the moment he was able.

Chapter Twenty-three

Candide and Martin reach the British coast, and what they see there

"Ah, Pangloss, Pangloss! Ah, Martin, Martin!" said Candide while they were proceeding on the Dutch ship. "What kind of world is this?"

"A mixture of mad and disgusting," Martin replied.

"You've been in England. Are they as crazy as the French?"

"It's a different kind of madness," said Martin. "You're aware that these two countries are at war, fighting over a few square acres of snow, somewhere in the vicinity of Canada, and that they've already spent, on this lovely scuffle, far more than the whole of Canada is worth. Telling you more precisely whether one country or the other contains a larger number of lunatics—well, I'm not smart enough for that. All I know is that, in general, the people we're going to see are extremely touchy."

As they were chatting, the ship reached Portsmouth. The banks were lined by immense multitudes, all staring at a stout man, his eyes blindfolded, kneeling on the deck of a Royal Navy ship. Four soldiers, standing around him, each proceeded—as peacefully as you'll ever see—to fire three shots into his head, after which the crowds went happily away.

"What is all this?" said Candide. "And what fiend out of hell wields this power, everywhere on earth?"

He asked who the fat man was, just killed with such elaborate ceremony.

"He's an admiral," people told him.

"And why did they kill this admiral?"

"Because he didn't kill enough people," said someone. "He fought a battle against a French admiral, and they decided he didn't get close enough."[4]

"But," said Candide, "the French admiral was just as far from the English admiral as the English admiral was from him!"

"Of course," someone said. "But in this country it's a good thing to kill an admiral, from time to time, to spur on the others."

Candide was so shocked, so stupefied, by what he had seen and heard, that he refused to so much as set a foot on English soil. He offered the Dutch captain whatever he wanted (and being Dutch, like the Surinam Dutch captain, he robbed Candide left and right) to take him, starting immediately, from there to Venice.

It took the captain two days to make the ship ready. They sailed

4. Admiral John Byng (1704–57) was executed in the manner and place and for the reasons stated.

down the coast of France and passed within sight of Lisbon. Candide shuddered. They sailed through the Gibraltar straits and then on into the Mediterranean Sea, and finally they arrived at Venice.

"God be praised!" said Candide, embracing Martin. "This is where I'll see Cunégonde! I trust Cacambo as I would myself. Everything is fine, everything's going well—everything's the best it could possibly be."

Chapter Twenty-four
Paquette and Friar Giroflée

As soon as they got to Venice, Candide hunted for Cacambo in every inn, every café; he visited all the whores and did not find him. Every day he got the latest information on all the ships, the boats, the barges: there was no news of Cacambo.

"How can this be?" he said to Martin. "I've had time to travel from Surinam to Bordeaux, go from Bordeaux to Paris, from Paris to Dieppe, from Dieppe to Portsmouth, down the French and Portuguese coasts, across the Mediterranean, then to spend several months in Venice, and my beautiful Cunégonde isn't here! All I've found, instead, is a fat strumpet and a Périgord priest! Cunégonde must be dead; there's nothing to do but die myself. Ah, it would have been better to stay in Eldorado than come back to this cursèd Europe! How right you were, my dear Martin! It's all mere illusion and disaster after disaster."

He fell into the blackest melancholy, paying no attention to brand-new operas or other carnival entertainments. No woman tempted him the least little bit.

Martin said:

"It's really foolish, expecting a half-breed valet with five or six million in his pockets to go looking for your mistress, hunting her all the way to the end of the earth, and then bringing her here to Venice. He'll take her for himself, if he finds her. If he doesn't find her, he'll take some other woman. My advice to you is: forget both your valet Cacambo and your mistress Cunégonde."

Martin was not consoling.

Candide's melancholy grew stronger, and Martin never stopped proving to him how little virtue there was on earth, and how little happiness, with the possible exception of Eldorado, to which no one could go.

Arguing about these important matters, and waiting, waiting for Cunégonde, Candide noticed a young monk with a girl on his arm. The monk was plump, lively, with a rosy complexion; his eyes were bright, his manner confident; he was handsome, he strutted rather than merely walking. The girl was very pretty, and was singing; she looked lovingly at her monk and, from time to time, pinched his full cheeks.

"You'll admit, at least," Candide said to Martin, "that those two are happy. Everyone I've ever found, until now, in all the populated parts of the world—except in Eldorado—is miserable. But seeing that girl and her monk, I'd bet these are two really happy."

"I'd bet they're not," said Martin.

"Let's ask them to dinner," said Candide, "and you'll see if I'm wrong."

They immediately approached the pair, greeted them, then invited them to sup on spaghetti with Lombard partridges and caviar, in the dining room at their lodgings, drinking such wines as Montepulciano, and Lacrima Christi, and Cyprian, and Samian. The young lady blushed, the monk agreed to join them, and the girl followed, looking surprised, confused, and sometimes shedding tears. They had no sooner walked into Candide's lodgings (her monk enjoying a drink, while he waited for them in the dining room) when she said:

"So! Mister Candide no longer recognizes Paquette!"

Candide, who had not been paying her much attention, since his thoughts were only of Cunégonde, said:

"Ah, my poor child. So it was you who brought Doctor Pangloss to such a fine state."

"Alas, sir, it was me," said Paquette. "I see you've been told the whole story. I've heard the terrible things that happened at Thunder-den-tronckh—the Baroness, Miss Cunégonde. But my fate's been no less miserable. I was a complete innocent, when you knew me. My confessor, a friar, had no trouble seducing me. And what followed was frightful. Not long after the Baron drove you off, kicking your backside so violently, I too was sent away. If a famous physician hadn't taken pity on me, I'd have been dead. Out of sheer gratitude, I was for quite a while his mistress. His wife was crazed with jealousy and used to beat me mercilessly, day after day. She was a real wild woman. He was the ugliest man in the world, and I was the most miserable of creatures, being beaten like that on account of a man I didn't love.

"I'm sure you know how risky it can be, for shrewish women, to be married to doctors. This one was outraged by his wife's behavior and, one day, to cure her of a little cold, gave her a medicine so potent that she died two hours later, after frightful convulsions. Her family brought criminal charges; he ran off, and I was thrown in jail. Being innocent wouldn't have saved me, if I hadn't been rather pretty. The judge set me free, on condition that he assume the doctor's place. It wasn't long before he found someone he liked better, and I was kicked out, empty-handed, so I had to keep on with this awful business, which strikes you men as wonderfully pleasant, but to us is simply a pit of horrors.

"I came to Venice to practice my trade. Ah, sir, if you only knew what it's like, having to fondle, all without feeling, first an old merchant, then a lawyer, a monk, a gondolier, a priest—constantly open to insults and indignities, often reduced to borrowing a skirt so you can go out and find some disgusting man to lift it up, having one of them steal what another one gives you, being fleeced by policemen, and looking forward to nothing but a frightful old age, a poorhouse, and then a dunghill—ah, if you only knew, you'd realize I'm one of the most miserable creatures in the world."

Paquette thus opened her heart, in Candide's rooms, and in the presence of Martin, who said:

Chapter Twenty-four

"Ah, I've already won half the bet."

"Still," said Candide to the girl, "you seemed so cheerful, so joyful, when I first saw you, here in Venice. You were singing, you were fondling the monk quite naturally and willingly: you seemed to me just as happy as you say, now, you're unhappy."

"Ah, sir," replied Paquette, "that's another of this profession's miseries. Yesterday I was beaten and robbed by a policeman, and today I have to appear cheerful, so I can please this monk."

Candide needed to hear no more; he admitted that Martin had been right. They went to the dining room and sat down with Paquette and the monk. The conversation was lively enough, and by the time they'd finished the meal they were chatting on good terms.

"My Father," said Candide to the monk, "it seems to me you enjoy the kind of life everyone might envy. Your face glows with good health, your countenance proclaims happiness; you have an exceedingly pretty girl to amuse you; and you seem perfectly at ease in your monkish existence."

"By God," said Father Giroflée, "I could wish every monk in my order to the bottom of the ocean. I've been tempted, a hundred times, to set fire to our monastery and go off and become a Turk. I was fifteen when my family forced me to put on these disgusting garments, so they could leave still more money to my damned older brother—may God strike him down! The monastery's full of jealousy, quarrels, anger. Yes, I've preached a couple of stupid sermons, and they've brought in a little cash, half of which the prior stole; the rest goes for girls. But at night, when I go back to the monastery, I'm ready to smash my head open on our dormitory walls, and all my colleagues feel the same way."

Turning to Candide, with his usual composure, Martin said:

"Well. Haven't I won the whole bet?"

Candide gave Paquette two thousand in gold and the monk a thousand.

"Let me tell you," he said, "this will make them happy."

"I don't believe it for a minute," said Martin. "Your money might just as well make them even more miserable than they were."

"It might very well," said Candide. "But there's one thing that comforts me: I see that we often come across people we never expected to see again. It could happen that, having gotten back my red sheep, and Paquette, I'll also find Cunégonde."

"I hope," said Martin, "that she will make you happy, some day, but I seriously doubt it."

"How harsh you are," said Candide.

"Because I've lived," said Martin.

"Just look at the gondoliers," said Candide. "Don't they sing all the time?"

"You don't see them at home," said Martin, "with their wives and all their brats. The Doge of Venice has his sorrows, the gondoliers have theirs. It's true that, all things considered, the gondolier is better off than the Doge. But the difference remains so insignificant it's not worth the trouble of talking about."

"People talk," said Candide, "of Senator Pococuranté, who lives in that handsome palace on the shore of the Brenta, and who often welcomes foreigners. They claim he's never known sorrow."

"I should like to meet so rare a specimen," said Martin.

Candide promptly sent a note to Lord Pococuranté, asking his consent for a visit the very next day.

Chapter Twenty-five
Visit to Lord Pococuranté, a nobleman of Venice

Candide and Martin took a gondola and went along the Brenta to Senator Pococuranté's palace. His estate stretched in all directions, and his gardens were decorated with handsome marble statues; the architecture of his palace was splendid. The master of the house, a man of sixty, immensely wealthy, received his pair of curious visitors most politely but not very cordially, which troubled Candide and did not in the least displease Martin.

Two pretty girls, well and properly dressed, served them cups of chocolate fairly foaming with whipped cream. Candide could not keep from praising their beauty, their graciousness, and their swift efficiency.

"They're all right," said Senator Pococuranté. "I take them to my bed, sometimes, because I've grown terribly weary of Venetian ladies with their petty little games, their incessant jealousy and quarreling and moods, their pettiness and pride, and their stupidity, and all the poems you have to make (or commission) for them. Yet, in the end, I'm really getting weary of these two girls, too."

Having finished their chocolate, Candide and Martin walked through a long gallery, distinctly startled by the beautiful paintings. Candide asked which of the great masters had been responsible for the first two, in particular.

"They're by Raphael," said the Senator. "I bought them some years ago, from sheer pride; they were exceedingly expensive. They're supposed to be the most beautiful in all Italy, but I don't like them a bit. The pigments have gone quite dark; the faces aren't clear enough, and they don't stand out at all; he hasn't painted the dresses so they look like real cloth; and in a word, no matter what people say, for me they're simply not a true representation of nature. I don't like pictures unless they show me nature as it truly is, and there aren't any like that. I have a lot of paintings, but I no longer look at them."

While they were waiting for dinner, Pococuranté had chamber music played for them. Candide was delighted.

"Noise like this," said Pococuranté, "can be entertaining for half an hour. But if it lasts much longer, the whole world gets tired, though nobody's brave enough to admit it. These days, music is simply the art of performing difficult pieces, and that which is merely difficult, and which goes on and on, cannot be pleasing.

"I might prefer opera, on the whole, if they hadn't learned how to make it monstrous, which revolts me. That may appeal to those who like bad tragedies set to music, where so-called drama is only a device—usually managed most clumsily, and even irrelevantly—to bring in two or three ridiculous songs that show off some actress's vocal cords. Let anyone who likes such stuff—or who's able to endure it—gape and swoon with pleasure, watching a eunuch hum the role of Caesar or Cato, and stumbling awkwardly around on the stage. Myself, I long ago gave up such banal shabbiness, which has now become the glory of Italy, and for which our rulers pay so extravagantly."

Candide argued a bit, but discreetly. Martin was completely of the Senator's opinion.

They sat down to dinner and, after an excellent meal, were shown into the Senator's library. Candide, seeing a magnificently bound volume of Homer, praised the good taste of his illustrious host.

"This," he said, "this is a book that thrilled great Pangloss, the best philosopher in all Germany."

"It's not a book that does the same for me," said Pococuranté coldly. "Once upon a time, I was forced to delude myself, believing I delighted in reading Homer. But the constant repetition of battles, every one just like the other; and those gods, forever in motion but never actually doing anything; that Helen, for whom the war was fought but who barely has a walk-on role in the whole poem; that Trojan city, which is forever besieged and never captured; all this produced in me deadly, deadly boredom. I'd occasionally inquire of scholars whether Homer's poems bored them as much as they bored me. The honest men among them admitted it: the book kept falling out of their hands. But they always had to have it in their libraries, like a monument of antiquity, or like those battered and mildewed old coins that you can't use like real money."

"Surely Your Excellency doesn't feel that way about Virgil," said Candide.

"I agree," said Pococuranté, "that the second, fourth, and sixth book of his *Aeneid* are excellent. But as for pious, dutiful Aeneas, and big, strong Cloanthus, and faithful Achates, and tiny little Ascanius, and that imbecilic King Latinus with his bourgeois wife, Queen Amatus, and that insipid Lavinia—I don't think there's anything more stilted and distasteful. I'd rather read Tasso, and Ariosto's cock-and-bull stories."

"May I be presumptuous and ask you, sir, if you don't take delight in reading Horace?"

"There are some epigrams," said Pococuranté, "which a man of the world can find useful and which, having been wrapped in spirited verse, are easier to memorize. But I don't much care for his trip to Brindisium, and his description of a bad dinner, and the pickpockets' quarrel, between someone called Pupilus,[5] whose language, we're told, 'was full of pus,' and somebody else, whose language 'was like vinegar.' Horace's obscene poems attacking old women and witches, frankly, I read with utter disgust. Nor do I see the merit of telling his friend Maecenas that if *he* thinks Horace a first-class poet, Horace will bang his forehead against the stars. Fools admire everything a

---

5. Rupilius: "Rupilus Rex, the outlaw," *Satires* I.7.

poet of reputation writes. I read only for myself; what I love is only what I can use."

Candide, who had not been raised ever to judge anything for himself, was astonished to hear such things; Martin found Pococuranté's way of thinking entirely reasonable.

"Oh, here's a volume of Cicero," said Candide. "Now there's a great man you probably never stop reading."

"I've never read him," said the Venetian. "What difference does it make to me if he was Cluentius's lawyer, or Rabirius's? I've got my hands full with cases *I* have to judge. I'd have been more comfortable with his philosophical writing, but I realized he doubted everything, and I decided I knew just as much as he did, and in order to be ignorant I didn't need anybody's help."

"Ah!" exclaimed Martin. "Here are eighty volumes, the proceedings of an academy of science. Maybe there are worthwhile things in here."

"There ought to be," said Pococuranté, "if a single author, in all of this rubbish, had invented even a way of manufacturing pins. But nowhere in any of these fat books is there anything but useless schemes, and absolutely nothing of any use."

"Ah, what a lot of drama you have!" said Candide. "In Italian, in Spanish, in French!"

"Yes," said the Senator, "there are three thousand, and not three dozen worth a thing. As for all those volumes of sermons, the whole lot not worth a single page of Seneca, and all those heavy theological tomes, you'd be right if you imagined I never opened them—neither I nor anyone else."

Martin saw shelves loaded with English books.

"I suspect," he said, "that any man who considered himself a republican must be pleased by most of these, written so freely."

"Yes," said Pococuranté. "It's good to write exactly what one thinks: that is every man's right. Here in our Italy, no one writes anything except what he doesn't think. Those who dwell in the land of Caesars and Antonine emperors don't dare have an idea without an inquisitor's permission. I'd be satisfied with the kind of freedom these English geniuses enjoyed, and profited from, if political passion and spirit didn't corrupt everything worthwhile in that precious freedom."

Seeing a volume of Milton, Candide asked if the Senator considered him a great man.

"Who?" said Pococuranté. "That barbarian, author of a long commentary on the first chapter of Genesis, in ten books of stony-hard verse? That vulgar imitator of the Greeks, who defaced Creation and, despite Moses showing us the Eternal One making the world by means of words, has the Messiah plucking a giant compass out of a cabinet, in order to outline his work? How could I approve of a man who corrupted Tasso's hell and his Satan? Who sometimes disguised Lucifer as a toad, and sometimes as a pygmy, and makes him repeat the same speech a hundred times, and even argue theology? Who took seriously Ariosto's comic account of the invention of firearms, then had the devils shooting off cannon in heaven? Neither I, nor indeed anyone in Italy, could take pleasure in such dismal extravagance. Having Sin and Death marry, and Sin give birth to snakes, would make men of even mildly refined taste simply throw up, and his interminable description of a hospital could only appeal to a gravedigger. Milton's obscure, bizarre, disgusting poem was despised from the start; I view it, today, exactly as his contemporaries saw it, in his own country. Anyway, I say what I think, and I don't care in the least whether others think the same way."

Candide was upset by this speech; he respected Homer, and he rather liked Milton.

"Alas!" he whispered to Martin. "I'm afraid this fellow must be completely contemptuous of our German poets."

"There wouldn't be anything so bad about that," said Martin.

"O what a high and mighty man!" Candide went on, between his teeth. "What a great genius, this Pococuranté! He approves of nothing."

Having now finished their inspection of his books, they went down to the garden. Candide lavished praise on its beauties.

"I cannot imagine anything in worse taste," said the Senator. "All we've got here are geegaws. But starting tomorrow, I'm going to have all this planted according to a far grander pattern."

When his two curious visitors had said farewell to His Excellency:

"Now that," Candide told Martin, "should convince you that here is the happiest man in the world, since he stands so far above everything he owns."

"Don't you understand," said Martin, "that he's disgusted with everything he owns? As Plato declared, a long time ago, the best stomachs are not the ones that refuse all food."

"Still," said Candide, "doesn't he enjoy criticizing everything, perceiving flaws where other men think they see only beauty?"

"In short," said Martin, "he takes pleasure in not having pleasure?"

"Oh well," said Candide. "No one's as happy as I'll be, when I get to see Miss Cunégonde."

"To have hope is always good," said Martin.

But days, and weeks, kept rolling by; Cacambo never showed up; and Candide was so steeped in sadness that he didn't notice how Paquette and Friar Giroflée had not even bothered, out of gratitude, to pay him a visit.

Chapter Twenty-six
A dinner that Candide and Martin shared with six foreigners, and who they were

One night, when Candide, accompanied by Martin, shared a dinner table with six foreigners who lodged in the same hostelry, a dark-skinned man came up behind him and, taking him by the arm, said:

"Be ready to leave when we do—without fail."

Candide turned around and saw Cacambo. Only the sight of

Cunégonde could have more astonished and better pleased him. He was almost mad with joy, and embraced his dear friend.

"Surely, Cunégonde is here too? Where is she? Take me to her, so I can die of happiness in her company."

"Cunégonde is not here," said Cacambo. "She's in Constantinople."

"Ah, God! In Constantinople! But even if she were in China, I'd fly there. Let's go."

"We'll be leaving after dinner," said Cacambo. "I can't tell you any more: I'm a slave, my master is waiting for me. I have to go and serve him his supper. Don't say a word. Eat and be ready."

Torn between joy and sadness, Candide, thrilled at seeing his faithful agent, was astonished that Cacambo was a slave, and wholly caught up at the thought of recovering his mistress; his heart was beating wildly, his mind at sixes and sevens. He sat himself down to eat dinner with Martin (who was totally unperturbed by whatever was going on) and with six foreigners who had just come from the Carnival of Venice.

Cacambo, pouring wine for one of these six, bent to his master's ear, as the meal ended, and said:

"Sire, Your Majesty can leave whenever you wish to: the ship is ready."

After saying this, he disappeared. The astonished guests were looking at one another, absolutely silent, when another servant came over to his master and said:

"Sire, Your Majesty's carriage is at Padua, and the boat is waiting."

The master gestured; the servant vanished. Once more, the guests stared back and forth, and everyone's surprise was doubled. Then a third servant came to yet another foreigner and said:

"Sire, trust me: Your Majesty should not linger here. I'll go make everything ready."

And he too disappeared.

At this point, Candide and Martin had no doubt this was not simply another Carnival masquerade. A fourth servant spoke to a fourth master:

"Your Majesty can leave whenever you wish," and left just as the others had.

A fifth servant spoke to a fifth master.

But the sixth servant spoke quite differently to the sixth foreigner, who was seated near Candide:

"By God, Your Majesty, they're refusing to extend you any further credit, and refusing it to me as well, so we might very well get thrown in the jug tonight—both of us. So I'm off to take care of myself. Farewell."

All six servants having gone, the six foreigners, together with Candide and Martin, sat in the most profound silence. It was finally broken by Candide:

"Gentlemen," he said, "this is an odd joke. How come you're all kings? Speaking for myself, and for Martin, I confess we're neither of us the least bit royal."

Cacambo's master was the first to reply, speaking seriously, in Italian:

"I'm not in the least jesting. My name is Achmed the Third.[6] For some years I was Grand Sultan. I had dethroned my brother; my nephew dethroned me; my ministers had their heads chopped off; I live out my days in an abandoned seraglio. My nephew, Grand Sultan Mahmoud, sometimes allows me to travel abroad for my health, and I came to spend the Carnival season in Venice."

Then a young man seated near Achmed spoke, saying:

"My name is Ivan the Sixth; I was Emperor of all the Russias. I was dethroned in my cradle; my father and mother were locked up; I was raised in prison. I sometimes have permission to travel, accompanied by those who watch over me, and I came to spend the Carnival season in Venice."

The third man said:

"I am Charles Edward, King of England; my father yielded his throne to me and I fought to maintain it. They ripped the hearts out of eight hundred of my supporters, then threw them in their faces. I was sent to prison; I came to Rome to visit my father, the King, who was dethroned exactly as I have been, and as his father was, and I am in Venice to spend the Carnival season."

Then the fourth man spoke:

"I am the King of Poland; the luck of war deprived me of my hereditary rights, exactly as my father had been. I am resigned to the will of Providence, as are Sultan Achmed, Emperor Ivan, and King

6. The stories of these deposed rulers are all actual cases.

Charles Edward, and may God grant long life to all of them; and I came to spend the Carnival season in Venice."

The fifth man said:

"I too was King of Poland; I lost my throne twice; but Providence has given me another state to rule, and I have done more good, there, than all the Slav kings, along the banks of the Vistula, have ever been able to do. I too am resigned to the will of Providence, and have come to spend the Carnival season in Venice."

The sixth and last ruler spoke:

"Gentlemen, I am not quite so great a lord as the rest of you, but most certainly I have been a king just as you have been. I am Theodore; I was chosen King of Corsica; I have been addressed as 'Your Majesty,' although at the moment I am not always addressed as 'sir.' I have had coinage minted, but I no longer possess a red cent; I had two secretaries of state, but I barely have a valet; I have sat on a throne, and I have been rather a long time in London, lying on straw. I am seriously concerned about being treated in the same fashion, here, although like Your Majesties I came to spend the Carnival season in Venice."

The other five kings listened to this speech with noble compassion. Each of them gave King Theodore twenty gold ducats, so he could dress himself and wear shirts, and Candide gave him a diamond worth two thousand gold ducats.

"Who can this be," said the five other kings, "this ordinary private citizen, who has the means to give a hundred times as much as we have done, and does indeed give that much? Are you too a king, sir?"

"No, nor do I have any interest in being one."

They had no sooner risen from the table when the hostel received, as paying guests, yet another four Serene Highnesses who, by the fortunes of war, had also lost their thrones and who had come to spend the rest of the Carnival season in Venice. But Candide paid no attention at all to these newcomers. All he thought about was going to Constantinople, to find his dear Cunégonde.

Chapter Twenty-seven
Candide's journey to Constantinople

Faithful Cacambo had already arranged, with the Turkish captain who was taking Sultan Achmed back to Constantinople, that Candide and Martin would also be welcomed on the ship. And so they came on board, having first prostrated themselves before His Miserable Highness. Along the way, Candide had said to Martin:

"There you have six dethroned kings, with whom we dined, and yet I gave alms to one of them. There may be many other kings even unluckier. Me, all I've lost was a hundred sheep, and I'm flying right into Cunégonde's arms. My dear Martin: once again, Pangloss was right. Everything is for the best."

"May it be so," said Martin.

"Still," said Candide, "what we've just experienced, in Venice, was terribly unlikely. Who has ever seen, or heard of, six dethroned kings sitting down to dinner at an inn?"

"It's no more extraordinary," said Martin, "than most of the things that have happened to us. Kings are often dethroned; it's quite usual. And as far as the honor of dining with them—that is a mere trifle, not worth a second thought."

Candide was no sooner on board the ship than he flung his arms around his friend and onetime valet, Cacambo.

"So!" he said. "How is Cunégonde? Still prodigiously beautiful? Does she still love me? How is she behaving? You've surely bought her a palace in Constantinople?"

"My dear master," replied Cacambo. "Cunégonde is washing dishes on the shores of the Sea of Marmara, for a prince who has very few dishes; she's a household slave for an old, exiled prince named Ragotski, who gets a pension of three shillings a day from the Sultan. But what's even sadder, she's lost her looks and has become horribly ugly."

"Ah!" said Candide. "Beautiful or ugly, I'm an honorable man and my duty is to love her forever. But how could she fall so low, with the five or six million you brought with you?"

"Fine," said Cacambo. "Didn't I have to give two million to Señor Don Fernando d'Ibaraa, y Figueora, y Mascarenes, y Lampoudos, y Souza, Governor at Buenos Aires, for agreeing to let me have Miss Cunégonde? And didn't a bold pirate steal all the rest? And didn't this pirate take us to Cape Matapan, and to Milo, Nicaris, Samos, Petra, the Dardanelles, Marmora, and Scutari? Cunégonde and the old woman serve the prince, the one I told you about, and I'm the slave of a dethroned sultan."

"What a hideous chain of calamities, one after the other!" said Candide. "But no matter: I still have some diamonds; I won't have any trouble freeing Cunégonde. It's a pity she's become so ugly."

Then he turned to Martin:

"Who," he asked, "do you think has the most to complain of, Emperor Achmed, Emperor Ivan, King Charles Edward—or me?"

"I have no idea," said Martin. "I'd have to be in your hearts, before I could say."

"Ah!" said Candide. "If Pangloss were here, he'd know, and he'd tell us."

"I don't know," said Martin, "in what scales your Pangloss could weigh men's misery and judge your sorrow. All I can guess is that there are millions of men on earth with a hundred times as much to complain about as King Charles Edward, Emperor Ivan, and Sultan Achmed."

"That may very well be so," said Candide.

In a few days they reached the Black Sea strait, known as the Bosporus. Candide began by purchasing Cacambo's freedom, at a singularly high price, and then, without losing a moment, he jumped into a galley ship, together with his companions, to seek the shores of the Sea of Marmara, to search for Cunégonde—however ugly she might have become.

Among the men rowing the galley, there were two convicts who handled the oars very poorly, and the Levantine captain repeatedly applied his beef-hide whip to their bare shoulders. Inevitably, Candide looked at them more carefully than he did the other rowers and, feeling pity for their plight, stepped a bit closer. There was something about their distorted faces that, to his mind, seemed to more or less resemble Pangloss and that unlucky Jesuit, the Baron, Miss Cunégonde's brother. The notion affected and saddened him. He looked at them even more carefully.

"Really," he said to Cacambo, "if I hadn't seen Pangloss hanged, and if I hadn't had the ill luck of killing the Baron, I'd think that here they were, rowing in this galley."

Hearing the words "Pangloss" and "Baron," the two convicts let out a loud shout, sat motionless on their rowing bench, and dropped their oars. The Levantine captain rushed over, and the beef-hide whip swung fast and hard.

"Stop, stop, sir!" cried Candide. "I'll pay you whatever you want!"

"My God! It's Candide!" exclaimed one of the convicts.

"My God! It's Candide!" said the other one.

"Am I dreaming?" said Candide. "Am I awake? Am I here in this galley? Is this the noble Baron I killed? Is this Doctor Pangloss, who I saw hanged?"

"It's us, it's us," they answered.

"What! It's that great philosopher?" said Martin.

"Sir, my dear Levantine captain," said Candide, "how much ransom do you want for Baron Thunder-den-tronckh, one of the leading noblemen of Europe, and Doctor Pangloss, Germany's greatest philosopher?"

"You Christian dog," replied the Levantine captain, "since these two convict Christian dogs are barons and philosophers, which are surely positions of high worth in their countries, you'll pay me fifty thousand gold ducats."

"And you'll have it, sir. Row me to Constantinople, swift as lightning, and you'll be paid on the spot. But no: take me to Miss Cunégonde."

The captain had immediately swung the galley around, and had his men rowing for Constantinople faster than a bird can fly through the air.

Candide had embraced the Baron and Pangloss a hundred times.

"And how come I didn't kill you, my dear Baron? And my dear Pangloss, how can you still be alive, having been hanged? And why are you both in a Turkish galley?"

"Is it true that my dear sister is here in this land?" said the Baron.

"Yes," answered Cacambo.

"And here I see my dear Candide," exclaimed Pangloss.

Candide introduced them to Martin and Cacambo. Everyone embraced everyone else; they were all talking at the same time.

The galley flew; they had reached Constantinople. They paid a visit to a Jew to whom, for fifty thousand gold ducats, Candide sold a diamond worth a hundred thousand, though the Jew swore in the name of Abraham that he could not pay a cent more. Candide immediately ransomed Pangloss and the Baron, the former of whom threw himself at his liberator's feet, weeping for joy; the latter thanked him with a nod, promising to repay him just as soon as the opportunity presented itself.

"But is it really possible my sister is here in Turkey?" he said.

"Nothing is more possible," said Candide, "since she's washing dishes for a Transylvanian prince."

He at once sent for two Jews and sold them more diamonds, after which they hired another galley and went to free Cunégonde.

Chapter Twenty-eight

What happened to Candide, Cunégonde, Pangloss, Martin, etc.

"I beg your pardon, yet again," Candide said to the Baron. "Forgive me, Reverend Father, for having run a sword through your body."

"Let's say no more about it," said the Baron. "I was a bit too hasty, I admit it. But since you'd like to know what accident allowed you to see me in the galleys, I'll tell you that after my wound had been healed, by the Apothecary Brother of my order, I was attacked and carried off by a Spanish raiding party. They threw me into a Buenos Aires prison just after my sister left there. I asked to be sent back to Rome, in custody of our Jesuit Father General. I was sent to Constantinople, to serve as the French Ambassador's charitable administrator. I had served in that capacity for only eight days when, one night, I happened on a young seraglio attendant, a remarkably well-made fellow. The weather was extremely warm; the young man decided to take a bath; I decided to take one, too. I was not aware that a Christian found naked with a young Muslim was guilty of a capital offense. An Islamic judge ordered that I have a hundred blows on the soles of my feet, and then be sent to the galleys. I don't think any greater injustice could have been perpetrated.

"But I'd like to know why my sister is kitchen maid to a Transylvanian prince, an exile in Turkey."

"But you, my dear Pangloss," said Candide, "how can I be seeing you once more?"

"It's true," said Pangloss, "that you saw me hanged, and of course I was to be burned at the stake. But as you recall, it began to rain torrentially, just as they were about to roast me. The storm was so violent they could not light a match. So, not being able to do anything more, they hanged me. A surgeon bought my body, took me home, and began to dissect me, starting with a crisscross incision from navel to clavicle. No one could have been less adequately hanged than I had been. The Chief Executioner of the Holy Inquisition, a subdeacon, was in fact a superb roaster of human beings, but he did not do much in the way of hanging. The rope was wet and sticky, so it knotted up—and, in a word, I went on breathing. The crisscross incision made me scream so loudly that my surgeon fell over backward, and convinced that he'd been dissecting a devil, he fled in terror, falling once again on the staircase. His wife heard the noise and came running; she'd been in an adjoining room. She saw me stretched out on the table, with my crisscross incision, and was even more terrified than her husband. She ran for her life, and fell right on top of him. When they were beginning to come to themselves, I heard the wife say to her husband:

" 'My dear, what made you take it into your head to dissect a heretic? Don't you know that these people's bodies are always possessed by the devil? I'm going to hurry off and find a priest to exorcise him.'

"Hearing this, I shuddered, and collecting what strength I had left, I cried:

" 'Have pity on me!'

"At last, this Portuguese barber plucked up his courage; he sewed me up; even his wife took care of me; I was back on my feet in two weeks. The barber found me a job, and I entered the service of a Knight of Malta who was traveling to Venice. But my master had run out of money and couldn't pay me, so I hired myself out to a Venetian merchant, and accompanied him to Constantinople.

"One day, I made up my mind to go look at a mosque. It was empty except for an old imam and a very good-looking young worshipper who was saying her rosaries. Her breasts were almost bared, and between her tits she had a lovely bouquet of tulips, roses, anemones, buttercups, hyacinths, and primroses; her bouquet fell out; I picked it up and, with the most respectful zeal, put it back for her. It took me so long to get it back in place that the imam got angry and, seeing that I was a Christian, called for help. I was brought to an

Islamic judge, who ordered me to have a hundred blows on the soles of my feet and then sent to the galleys. I was taken to the same galley, and chained to the same rowing bench, as the Baron.

"There were also four young men from Marseille on this galley, and five Neapolitan priests, and two Corfu monks, who told us that these things happened all the time. The Baron claimed he'd been far more unjustly dealt with; for my part, I claimed it was much more permissible to replace a bouquet on a woman's bosom than to be naked with a seraglio servant. We argued constantly, and we both got twenty blows of the beef-hide whip every day, when the interlocking sequence of events, in this universe, brought you to our galley, so you could ransom us."

"Well! My dear Pangloss," Candide said to him. "When you were being hanged, dissected, beaten with a stick, and rowing in the galleys, did you always believe that everything was for the best in this best of all worlds?"

"I remain faithful to my basic beliefs," said Pangloss, "because, in the end, I remain a philosopher. It wouldn't be right for me disown myself; Leibniz cannot have been wrong; and our world's pre-existent harmony, furthermore, is the loveliest thing there is, along with the fullness of space and the *materia subtilis*, or subtlety of matter."

Chapter Twenty-nine

How Candide found Cunégonde and the old woman

While Candide, the Baron, Pangloss, Martin, and Cacambo were recounting their adventures and arguing whether what takes place in this universe comes about by chance or according to some plan, and about causes and effects, and about physical and moral evil, and about free will and necessity, and about the solace one can find when rowing in Turkish galleys, they reached the shores of the Sea of Marmara and the dwelling of the Transylvanian prince. And the very first things they saw were Cunégonde and the old woman, who were hanging towels out to dry.

The Baron turned pale at the sight. Soft-hearted, loving Candide, seeing his lovely Cunégonde burned brown by the sun, her eyes red and sore, her breasts flattened, her cheeks wrinkled, her arms roughened and scaly, took three horrified steps back, and then came toward her, propelled by the power of good manners. She embraced Candide and her brother; everyone embraced the old woman; and Candide ransomed them both.

Not far away, there was a small farm. The old woman suggested settling themselves there, while they waited to see what fate might bring them. Cunégonde did not know she'd become ugly, no one having told her: she reminded Candide of his promises, her tone so clear and firm that the good-hearted fellow was afraid to refuse her. So he told the Baron he planned to marry his sister.

"Never!" said the Baron. "I will not endure so vulgar a thing from her, or such insolence from you. No one will ever accuse me of anything so disgraceful: my sister's children could not be recorded in the canon of German nobility. No, my sister will never marry anyone but an imperial baron."

Cunégonde threw herself down and bathed his feet in tears. He was immovable.

"You incredible maniac," Candide said to him, "I rescued you from the galleys, I paid your ransom, I paid your sister's ransom, she's been a dishwasher, she's ugly, out of the goodness of my heart I'm willing to marry her, and you're still trying to stop me! If I let my anger guide me, I'd kill you all over again."

"Go ahead and kill me again," said the Baron, "but while I'm alive, you're not marrying my sister."

Chapter Thirty
Conclusion

In his heart of hearts, Candide hadn't the slightest desire to marry Cunégonde. But the Baron's insolence made him determined on the marriage, and Cunégonde so pressured him that he could not refuse her. He consulted Pangloss, Martin, and his faithful Cacambo. Pangloss wrote a splendid legal summary, in which he proved that the Baron had no rights over his sister and that, according to all imperial law, she could certainly enter into a morganatic marriage with a commoner like Candide. Martin's advice was to throw the Baron into the ocean. Cacambo recommended bringing the Baron to the Levantine captain and consigning him back to the galleys, after which he'd surely be sent back to the Jesuit Father General, in Rome, by the very first ship. Cacambo's advice seemed best, a decision in which the old woman concurred. Nothing was said to the Baron's sister. The whole thing was managed at the expense of a bit of money, and they had the double satisfaction of trapping a Jesuit and wounding a German Baron's pride.

It would be quite natural to suppose that, after so many disasters, but now married to his mistress and living with philosophic Pangloss, philosophic Martin, sensible Cacambo, and the wise old woman and having, besides, carried so many diamonds away from the land of the ancient Incas, Candide would have led the pleasantest of lives. But he had been so bamboozled by moneylending sharks that all he had left was his small farm; his wife, becoming uglier every day, turned into an intolerable shrew; the old woman had become sickly and was always in a worse humor than Cunégonde. Cacambo, who worked in their vegetable garden and sold their vegetables in Constantinople, was overworked and exhausted, and cursed his bad luck. Pangloss was in despair, not being able to shine at some German university. Martin, however, was definitely of the opinion that life is bad no matter where you are; he accepted what came with great patience. Candide, Martin, and Pangloss sometimes argued matters metaphysical and moral. They frequently saw, passing under their farmhouse windows, boats bearing Turkish bureaucrats, pashas, and

Islamic judges, being sent in exile to Lemnos, Mitylene, and Erzerum. They would see other Islamic judges, pashas, and bureaucrats who took the place of those sent into exile, and who were then exiled in their turn. They saw heads neatly fixed on poles being brought to the Sultan's palace. Such sights caused an increase in their argumentative discussions, and when they did not argue, boredom hung so heavy on them that the old woman bluntly asked, one day:

"I should like to know which is worse, to be raped a hundred times by Negro pirates, to have one buttock cut off, to run a Bulgar gauntlet, to be flogged and hanged in an auto-da-fé, to be dissected, to row in a galley, to experience—finally—all the miseries we all have endured, or simply to stay here with nothing to do?"

"That's quite a question," said Candide.

Her asking the question created a host of new viewpoints, and Martin, in particular, decided that men were born to live either amid the convulsions of uncertainty or in the lethargies of boredom. Candide did not agree, but he was not totally certain. Pangloss admitted to having been afflicted with constant suffering—but, once having declared that everything was wonderful, he'd go on declaring it, though he didn't believe a word he was saying.

There was one thing that served to confirm Martin's detestable principles, to make Candide hesitate more than ever, and to embarrass Pangloss. What happened was, one day, they saw Paquette and Father Giroflée come to the farm, obviously extraordinarily destitute. It had not taken them long to consume their three thousand in gold; they had separated, come back together; they had quarreled, gone to prison; they had escaped; and in the end, Father Giroflée had indeed turned Turk. Everywhere they went, Paquette practiced her profession, and no longer earned anything from it.

"I warned you," Martin told Candide, "that your gifts would soon be dissipated and would only make them more miserable. You've thrown away millions, you and Cacambo, and you're not any happier than Paquette and Giroflée."

"Ah, ah!" said Pangloss to Paquette. "Heaven brought you here among us, my poor child! Do you realize I lost the tip of my nose because of you, and an ear and one eye? What have you come to! And what a world this is!!"

This new episode led them to philosophize more than ever.

There was a famous dervish in the neighborhood who was considered the best philosopher in Turkey. They went to consult him; Pangloss was the spokesman and said:

"Master, we've come to ask you why such a strange animal as man was ever created."

"Mind your own business," said the dervish. "Is this any of your concern?"

"But, Reverend Father," said Candide, "the world is full of terrible evils."

"What difference does it make," said the dervish, "whether there's evil or good? When His Majesty sends a ship to Egypt, does he worry whether the mice in that ship are comfortable?"

"So what should we do?" said Pangloss.

"Shut your mouths," said the dervish.

"I had fancied," said Pangloss, "we might have some small discussion with you about causes and effects, and the best of all possible worlds, the origins of evil, the true nature of the soul, and pre-existent harmony."

At these words, the dervish slammed the door in their faces.

While they were conducting this conversation, it became known that, in Constantinople, two ministers of state and a teacher of Muslim law had been strangled, and a number of their friends had been impaled on sharp stakes. For some hours, this dreadful event was discussed everywhere. Pangloss, Candide, and Martin, as they were returning to the farm, met an old man taking a breath of fresh air in front of his house, under an arbor of orange trees. Pangloss, who was as inquisitive as he was argumentative, asked him the name of the Islamic teacher, just strangled.

"I don't know anything about that," said the good old man, "nor have I ever known the name of any Muslim teacher or minister of state. I know absolutely nothing about this business. My assumption has always been that those who meddle in public affairs often meet a miserable death, and deserve it. I never inquire into anything that happens in Constantinople. It's enough for me to have the produce of my fields sent there and sold there."

Having spoken these words, he invited the three strangers into his house. His two daughters and two sons gave them several varieties of sherbet, made with their own hands, and beverages flavored with lemon-peel preserves, oranges, lemons, limes, pineapples, pistachios, and Mocha coffee—but not blended with wretched coffee from Batavia and the Indonesian islands. And then this good Muslim's daughters perfumed the beards of Candide, Pangloss, and Martin.

"You must be the proprietor," said Candide to the Turk, "of a vast and magnificent estate?"

"I own only twenty acres," the Turk replied. "I cultivate them with my children. Our labor keeps us from those three great evils: boredom, sin, and want."

Going home to his farm, Candide thought deeply about the Turk's words. He said to Pangloss and Martin:

"I think this good old man has a better life than any of the six kings with whom we've had the honor of breaking bread."

"Greatness," said Pangloss, "is very dangerous, according to all the philosophers, since in the end Eglon, Moabite king, was assassinated by Ehud; Absalom was hung by his own hair and run through by three spears; King Nadab, Jeroboam's son, was killed by Baasha, King Elah by Zimri, Ahaziah by Jehu, Athaliah by Jehoiada. Kings Joachim, Jeconiah, and Zedekiah became slaves. You are familiar, are you not, with how Croesus perished, and Astyages, Darius, Denys of Syracuse, Pyrrhus, Perseus, Hannibal, Jugurtha, Ariovistus, Caesar, Pompey, Nero, Otho, Vitellius, Domitian, Richard the Second of England, Edward the Second, Henry the Sixth, Richard the Third, Mary Stuart, Charles the First, the three French Henrys, Emperor Henry the Fourth? You know—"

"I also know," said Candide, "that we need to work our fields."

"You're right," said Pangloss, "because when men were placed in the Garden of Eden, they were set there *ut operaretur eum*—that is, so they might work. This proves that men are not born for resting."

"Let us work without thinking," said Martin. "That is the only way to make life bearable."

All the members of their small society participated in this praiseworthy plan, each working at what he or she could do best. Their small farm produced a great deal. Cunégonde was truly very ugly, but she made excellent pastry. Paquette did embroidery; the old woman was in charge of their linens. Even Father Giroflée made himself useful: he was an excellent carpenter, and actually became a respectable man. And Pangloss would sometimes say to Candide:

"Everything that happens, in this best of all possible worlds, is linked to everything else, because when it comes down to it, if you hadn't been driven out of a mansion, by savage kicks in the backside, on account of your love for Miss Cunégonde, and you hadn't been taken by the Inquisition, and gone all over America on foot, and hadn't run the Baron through with a sword, and hadn't lost all your wonderful Eldorado sheep, you wouldn't be eating, here and now, lemon-peel preserves and pistachios."

"That's well said," replied Candide, "but we need to work our fields."

Suggested Reading

Here is a tiny sample of distinctive scholarship in English. Readers who would like a sense of the field as a whole should consult the series *Studies on Voltaire and the Eighteenth Century*, edited by the Voltaire Foundation at Oxford, which has published several volumes a year for nearly forty years.

Betts, C. J. "Exploring Narrative Structures in *Candide*." *Studies on Voltaire and the Eighteenth Century* 314 (1993): 1–131.

Gay, Peter. *Voltaire's Politics: The Poet as Realist*. Princeton, N.J.: Princeton University Press, 1959.

Kors, Alan Charles, ed. *Encyclopedia of the Enlightenment*. 4 vols. New York: Oxford University Press, 2003.

Mason, Haydn. *Voltaire: A Biography*. Baltimore: Johns Hopkins University Press, 1981.

Pearson, Roger. *The Fables of Reason: A Study of Voltaire's "Contes Philosophiques."* Oxford: Clarendon Press, 1993.

Voltaire. *Political Writings.* Edited and translated by David Williams. Cambridge: Cambridge University Press, 1994.

Wootton, David. "Unhappy Voltaire, or 'I Shall Never Get Over It as Long as I Live.'" *History Workshop Journal* 50 (2000): 141–59.

———. "Introduction." In Voltaire, *Candide and Related Texts.* Translated by Wootton. Indianapolis, Ind.: Hackett, 2000.